SHELAGH RIXON

LISTENING
UPPER – INTERMEDIATE

OXFORD SUPPLEMENTARY SKILLS

SERIES EDITOR: ALAN MALEY

OXFORD UNIVERSITY PRESS

Oxford University Press
Great Clarendon Street, Oxford OX2 6DP

Oxford New York
Athens Auckland Bangkok Bogota Buenos Aires
Calcutta Cape Town Chennai Dar es Salaam
Delhi Florence Hong Kong Istanbul Karachi
Kuala Lumpur Madrid Melbourne Mexico City
Mumbai Nairobi Paris Sao Paulo Singapore
Taipei Tokyo Toronto Warsaw

and associated companies in
Berlin Ibadan

Oxford and *Oxford English* are trade marks of
Oxford University Press

ISBN 0 19 453420 0

© Oxford University Press 1987

First published 1987
Seventh impression 1998

No unauthorized photocopying

Set by Promenade Graphics Ltd, Cheltenham.

Printed in Hong Kong

Illustrations by:

Gill Elsbury
David Haldane

The publishers would like to thank the following for their
permission to reproduce photographs:

Ardea London
Aspect Picture Library
British Museum
Reg Davis, Royal Marsden Hospital
Mary Evans Picture Library
Farmers Weekly Picture Library
The Kobal Collection
Palmetto Technologies

Location photography by Rob Judges

Thanks to Rod Pryde of the British Council,
for his part in the 'Hot Stuff' interview.

CONTENTS

FOREWORD

This series covers the four skill areas of Listening, Speaking, Reading and Writing at four levels — elementary, intermediate, upper-intermediate and advanced. Although we have decided to retain the traditional division of language use into the 'four skills', the skills are not treated in total isolation. In any given book the skill being dealt with serves as the *focus* of attention and is always interwoven with and supported by other skills. This enables teachers to concentrate on skills development without losing touch with the more complex reality of language use.

Our authors have had in common the following principles, that material should be:

- creative — both through author-creativity leading to interesting materials, and through their capacity to provoke creative responses from students;
- interesting — both for their cognitive and affective content, and for the activities required of the learners;
- fluency-focused — bringing in accuracy work only in so far as it is necessary to the completion of an activity;
- task-based — rather than engaging in closed exercise activities, to use tasks with pay-offs for the learners;
- problem-solving focused — so as to engage students in cognitive effort and thus provoke meaningful interaction;
- humanistic — in the sense that the materials speak to and interrelate with the learners as real people and engage them in interaction grounded in their own experience;
- learning-centred — by ensuring that the materials promote learning and help students to develop their own strategies for learning. This is in opposition to the view that a pre-determined content is taught and identically internalized by all students. In our materials we do not expect input to equal intake.

By ensuring continuing consultation between and among authors at different levels, and by piloting the materials, the levels have been established on a pragmatic basis. The fact that the authors, between them, share a wide and varied body of experience has made this possible without losing sight of the need to pitch materials and tasks at an attainable level while still allowing for the spice of challenge.

There are three main ways in which these materials can be used:

- as a supplement to a core course book;
- as self-learning material. Most of the books can be used on an individual basis with a minimum of teacher guidance, though the interactive element is thereby lost.
- as modular course material. A teacher might, for instance, combine intermediate *Listening* and *Speaking* books with upper-intermediate *Reading* and elementary *Writing* with a class which had a good passive knowledge of English but which needed a basic grounding in writing skills.

This book contains fifteen units, (seventeen different listening passages) which have been designed to give students experience of a variety of speech styles. There is a range of exercises which will help students strengthen their language abilities and encourage them to apply useful strategies to the sorts of listening situation they might reasonably be expected to start coping with in real life.

INTRODUCTION TO THE TEACHER

The speech styles and listening situations are:

- informal conversations and discussions, particularly those involving the telling of a story and hearers' reactions to it;
- informative talks and interviews of the sort often heard on British radio or the BBC World Service.

Academic lectures are not covered, although the sort of information-extraction exercises given in this book may be relevant to developing the skills to apply to such lectures.

Features of the spoken language

These two main types of listening situation have been chosen because of their general usefulness to a wide variety of students. The exercises draw students' attention to features of English speech which it is useful for them to be able to handle, not only as listeners, but as participants in discussions or conversations.

Features such as interruption, capturing attention, hesitation, 'tone' of voice are brought into focus for the student as listener.

Work involving the other three skills

As speakers, readers, and writers, there are ample exercises for the students to do, aimed at either giving them a starting point from which to confront the listening with more confidence, as in the case of the pre-listening reading or discussion exercises, or providing consolidation or extension work after a listening passage has been tackled.

Work on grammar and vocabulary

Language work consists of both vocabulary and grammar exercises, some to be done before listening as part of the process of setting up expectations that will help the students with what they hear, others to be done after listening as consolidation of the language the students may have come across in the passage itself. Although the purpose of the listening passages is definitely not to act as a mere quarry for 'new language', the exercises nevertheless ensure that the 'language potential' of listening experiences is not ignored.

Helping students develop listening strategies

In many units there is also a section or sections on 'Hints on listening' which draw the students' attention openly to strategies they might

use, or features of the spoken language that they should listen for and which may help them make their burden less heavy. The likelihood that a speaker talking spontaneously will repeat himself is one example. This means that the student need not panic if he or she misses something the first time around.

Helping students 'hear' English more easily

Because many students listening to English have problems with *hearing* the words, let alone understanding them, there are sections devoted to techniques of helping students develop their ability to 'hear' better. Noticing the difference in pronunciation between stressed and unstressed syllables is a basic starting point, and various techniques are used to help students 'guess from the context' what the less distinctly pronounced words might be.

Allowing students to see a transcript of what they have listened to used to be anathema to many teachers. It can, however, be very useful: *after* the main listening exercises have been done, both as a means of supporting students' attempts to 'hear' better, and as a way of letting them study the language of what they have just heard at more leisure and in more depth.

Exercises such as 'Reading with rhythm' fall into the category of helping students 'hear' better. Exercises in which they listen with the transcript to underline examples of a particular language feature (e.g. hesitation noises) are an example of use of the transcript to help them study the language itself in more depth. For this reason the transcripts have been printed in the back of the book. Of course this poses the problem of the temptation to 'cheat' by looking at the transcript ahead of time. If, however, you can convince students that their listening lessons are *lessons* and not *tests*, that they are therefore not expected to get everything right first time and that you, the teacher, will not be checking their interim answers at every moment in an inquisitorial way, they should see the point and not go to the back of the book prematurely because they hope to impress you with their 100 per cent correct, first-time answers. In any case, since much of the work concerns the *way* in which words are said, which cannot be represented accurately on the printed page, they will be wasting their time!

Tasks to perform while listening

These are concerned with both *challenging* and *helping* the students extract the important information from what they hear. They are usually in the form of short questions, frameworks for note-taking or simple grids to fill in with the information required. The principle has been to ask the right questions using the fewest words possible, and to impose the least burden of writing possible upon the students. If, when they answer, students can demonstrate understanding by putting a tick in the right place, it is useless to ask them to write a whole sentence!

There is some progression through the course from heavily-guided information extraction questions towards those in which the student decides for him or herself what information he or she should write down. Guided note-taking thus takes its place alongside the grid-filling type exercises.

There is a table on page ix showing the type of listening texts and listening skills practised in each unit. It may also be useful to look at the general 'shape' of a listening lesson.

Each lesson has 3 main phases:

1   Pre-listening
2   Listening
3   Follow-up.

The purpose of Pre-listening work can be:

1   to arouse a general interest in the subject and increase motivation.
2   to provide some input, language or information, which will help the students understand the listening passage better.

The function of the Listening phase is:
to help the students get what is important out of the passage.

This does not mean *only* 'The *main* information'. A view of listening which contents itself with the students vaguely understanding the gist of what they have heard may be too superficial. Very often a detailed understanding is necessary. Imagine being happy with just 'understanding the gist' of what your doctor told you to do with a potentially dangerous new medicine! The listening exercises *can* therefore concern the main outlines of what is said, but are *also* likely to go on to challenge the student to listen for particular points which may require careful listening and detailed understanding.

The Follow-up phase has two main functions:

1   Consolidation, i.e. to allow students time to reflect on what they have heard and maybe to collect examples of language use that it may help them in future to be able to handle.
2   Extension, i.e. to use the listening passage as a starting point for other language work, discussion, further reading or written production.

Within these three phases the different exercises fit. A discussion for example may come in the Pre-listening or the Follow-up phase and its purpose will be different in each case.

Methodology of the book

The sequence of work for most exercises goes from the individual to the pair to the whole class mode. This is to ensure that students have the chance to make up their own minds (and are forced to try) by themselves initially. They then have the support of comparing their results with a colleague, rather than being directly interrogated by

the teacher. They also often have the stimulus that is derived from finding out that one's colleague has got a completely different answer from oneself! Students in this position are highly motivated to listen with great attention at the next opportunity in order to find out who was right and who was wrong.

A final check with the whole class is not always necessary, but it is an option that allows you to summarize the points you think are important as well as gaining a general impression of how the class fared with a particular exercise.

When there is discussion or re-telling to be done, it is often a good idea to let students work in pairs first so that they can practise and gain confidence for the greater strain that speaking to the rest of the class later puts upon them. Speaking to the rest of the class is worthwhile in spite of the strain because it is in this way that interesting similarities and differences between students' experiences or in their interpretations of a passage come to light.

Mode of working

The normal situation that is presupposed is a teacher with a cassette recorder that he or she controls, and the whole class listens to. Instructions to the students in this case such as 'Listen again if you want to' mean that you have to assess (or take a vote on) whether the class needs to hear a tape again.

In cases where there is a minilab or a full language laboratory available, you can use the course with it, provided the students have space to move out of the listening positions in order to meet their colleagues for the discussion and follow-up work. You need of course to make sure that the students have been trained to use the controls on their machines to the best advantage, so that they can decide for themselves how to work — using the pause and rewind buttons frequently, or simply playing the whole tape through and listening again.

Jigsaw work

Some of the units have been designed so that they can be used for jigsaw work. This means that you split the class into different groups and that each group hears only one recording out of a set. Members from different groups then meet to exchange information on what they heard, in order to build up a wider picture of the topic or story. In this course, the following recordings are 'combinable' for jigsaw work. Worksheets for these units have been included on page 89 and may be photocopied without a formal request for permission. (The rest of the book is under the normal copyright protection.)

1 Unit 5 (Home computers), Parts 1 and 2 may be listened to by two different groups. The information is essentially the same, but the circumstances in which it is given are very different, as are the personalities of the two main speakers.

2 **Unit 5 (Home computers)**, Parts 1 and/or 2 and **Unit 11 (My computer makes me sick!)** may be listened to by two or three different groups, the focus being on the benefits and the dangers of home computer use.

3 **Unit 8 (Bottoms up!) and Unit 15 (The tree climbers of Pompeii)** are spontaneous stories concerning either free or improvised food. The single worksheet allows the two groups of students to collect and share information about similar themes.

4 The recordings for **Unit 12 (Mummy dust)**, **Unit 13 (Scientific studies) and Unit 14 (Rameses II)** can be listened to simultaneously by three different groups, who then pool information before going on to hear the whole interview right through.

Map of the book

Unit	Title	Listening texts	Listening skills practised	Topic/theme
1	Cold toads	Monologue, informative, humorous	Listening for the main ideas Listening for detail Recognizing comparison Listening for unstressed words Listening/reading with the transcript Recognizing speaker's intentions	Toads — people's reactions to them, their place in folklore, their mating habits
2	Job stereotypes	1 Short monologues, expressing indignation, irritation or protest 2 Interview, informative	Listening for the main ideas Listening and note-taking Listening for detail Recognizing contrast	Job holders' complaints about popular images of their work Results of a survey into children's attitudes to different professions
3	Hot stuff	Conversation (two people), spontaneous story-telling	Listening for the main ideas Listening for specific vocabulary Recognizing speaker's way of talking	One person's experience of growing her own food
4	Old birds	1 Mini-dictation 2 Interview, informative 3 Intonation exercise	Mini-dictation Listening for detail Recognizing certainty and uncertainty Recognizing intonation	Longevity in the bird world

Unit	Title	Listening texts	Listening skills practised	Topic/theme
5	Home computers	1 Conversation (four people), spontaneous story-telling 2 Conversation (two people), spontaneous story-telling	Listening for the main ideas Listening and note-taking Listening for detail Recognizing speaker's way of talking	Experiences with a home computer
6	Glasses that hear	Interview, informative	Listening for the main ideas Listening for unstressed words	Devices to help the deaf and hard-of-hearing
7	A post-industrial industry	Discussion (two experts and a chairperson), informative — experts competing and in conflict	Listening for the main ideas Recognizing tone and attitude Listening for detail Recognizing hostility Judging performance Dictation	Malaysia's rubber industry — facts and figures, changes and innovation
8	Bottoms up!	Conversation (two people), spontaneous story-telling	Listening for the main ideas Listening for more detail Recognizing speaker's way of talking	Food for free
9	Art or technology?	Monologue, informative	Listening for the main information Listening and note-taking	A history of the cheese-making process
10	How disgusting!	1 Conversation (three people) 'capping' each other's stories 2 Traditional rhyme for reading with rhythm	Identifying the speakers Recognizing tone and intention Listening for detail Recognizing ways of capturing attention Listening/reading with the transcript	Different types of cheeses
11	My computer makes me sick!	Monologue, informative, giving advice	Listening for the main information Listening for detail	Health hazards involved in using computers
12	Mummy dust	Monologue, informative	Listening for the main ideas Listening for specific information Listening and note-taking Listening for the most important theme	Egyptology and an introduction to the idea of mummification

Unit	Title	Listening texts	Listening skills practised	Topic/theme
13	Scientific studies	Interview, informative	Listening for detail Listening for the main information	More detail on recent scientific investigation into mummies
14	Rameses II	1 Interview, informative 2 Poem for reading with rhythm	Listening for detail Listening and note-taking Listening for specific language Listening/reading with the transcript	The life and times of Rameses II and the adventures of his mummy
15	Tree climbers of Pompeii	Conversation (two people), spontaneous story-telling	Listening for the outline of a story Listening for detail Recognizing 'echoing' Recognizing surprise and puzzlement Listening/reading with the transcript	Pine-nut 'farming' in Italy

1 Cold toads

1 Pre-listening

Task 1 Vocabulary

This is a picture of a toad.

What is your reaction to it? Tick the answer you choose.

- ☐ positive
- ☐ negative
- ☐ mixed

Here are some positive and negative reactions you might have.
Choose some that are close to your own feelings, and add any more
that you want to.

positive	negative
amusement	disgust
interest	fear
affection	distaste
. . . .	. . . .
. . . .	. . . .

Task 2 Expressing reactions

Tell the rest of the class what your reactions to toads are, for
example

My usual reaction is one of | *amusement and interest.*
| *disgust.*
| *fear and distaste.*

Task 3   Discussion

Are there any stories or beliefs about toads in your country? Tell the rest of the class anything you know about toads.

Task 4   Reading

Read the text.

Frogs and toads (toads are the ones with the dry bumpy skin, and they don't *jump* like frogs do. They just walk.) appear in a lot of European legends and folk tales.

At one time people believed that toads had a precious stone hidden inside their heads.

In many stories a handsome prince is changed into a frog or a toad by a wicked witch or magician, and can only resume his human shape if a beautiful girl will kiss him. Since toads are not often particularly attractive to young women, the poor prince usually had to wait many years before an obliging girl overcame her distaste, kissed him and broke the spell. Her reward, of course, was the chance of marrying the handsome prince.

"At least you've got a chance. Whoever heard of a princess kissing a duck-billed platypus?"

Are there any similar stories from your culture of magic spells changing people into animals or birds?

Tell a partner about any story like this that you know, then tell the rest of the class, for example

In my country there's a story about a . . . . . . who is changed into a . . . . . . by a . . . .

2   Listening

The radio talk is about how ordinary toads (not disguised princes) try to make themselves more attractive. More precisely, it is about how male toads behave when they are looking for a mate.

Task 1   Predicting information

Try to guess some of the things the speaker might say. This will help you to understand more when you hear the passage.

Have you any ideas about what might make a male toad attractive (to a female toad, that is!).

Choose what you think is probable and add any ideas of your own.

- ☐ colour
- ☐ size
- ☐ smell
- ☐ texture of skin

. . . .

. . . .

. . . .

. . . .

Tell the rest of the class what you think.

Task 2   Getting the main ideas

▣ Do not worry about the detail at this stage. Listen straight through as often as you need in order to answer the questions below. Read the instructions carefully and make sure you understand what to do before you start.

This is a picture of a pond showing the temperature of the water in different places. The darker the colour, the colder it is. Mark the place where you would sit if you were a male toad looking for a mate.

According to the speaker, which of these three male toads would be the most attractive to a female (in the dark!)?

a 25°   b 25°   c 30°

Write the letters in the correct spaces.

most attractive . . . .

. . . .

least attractive . . . .

Check your answers in pairs and listen again if you want to.
Tell the rest of the class what you thought.

Task 3 Listening for detail

What exactly does the male toad do to make himself more attractive?
Listen again and fill in this chart to show the chain of cause and effect.

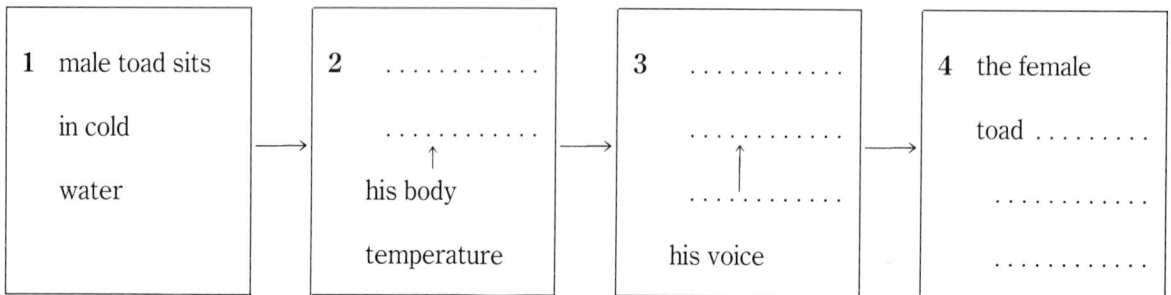

1 male toad sits in cold water	2 . . . . ↑ his body temperature	3 . . . . ↑ . . . . his voice	4 the female toad . . . .

3 Follow-up

Task 1   Expressing comparison

The passage is full of expressions of comparison, e.g.:

The bigger the toad, the deeper his croak.
A cold toad gives a deeper croak.

📼 Listen to the passage again and complete these sentences to collect
more examples

Many of the . . . . toads are forced right out of the pond and are

obliged to sit on the bank where (since it is . . . . out of the water

than in, even in North Carolina) the small toads' croaking becomes even

. . . . and . . . . enticing.

Task 2   Hearing exactly what the speaker says

a   Fill in the gaps to show the details about the research on toads
and where the speaker heard of it. The purpose of this exercise is to
give you practice in writing down unfamiliar names and words in
English.

The speaker heard about the research.

From L. . . . . who read it in The . . . . which

got it from Dr. . . . . of . . . . . . University, North Carolina

📼 **b**   Listen again and complete this extract from the end of the
passage with the words you hear. The purpose of this exercise is to
help you hear unstressed words more easily.

But there is still some consolation . . . . the warm weaklings. For in

order . . . . get into . . . . pond, the females do, ...

course, have . . . . run the gauntlet . . . . the bank: where,

says Dr Fairchild, ... small males make the most . . . .

their opportunities. It should not . . . . long before . . . .

large toads learn . . . . lurk on the bank and shut up.

Compare your answers in pairs and listen again if you want to. Then
check your answers by looking at the transcript on page 75.

Task 3 Reading with rhythm

📼 Now look again at the last section of the transcript on page 75. The syllables which the speaker stresses are underlined. Play this part of the tape again and read aloud, keeping time with the speaker. Trying to match your stresses to his stresses will help you!

Task 4 Recognizing intentions

📼 Listen again, if you want to, and give your impressions of the speaker's intentions when giving the talk, and the tone he uses. (You can choose more than one alternative in each case.)

Do you think he wanted to

☐ amuse
☐ instruct
☐ frighten
☐ disgust
☐ interest his listeners?

Is his tone

☐ serious
☐ shocked
☐ angry
☐ amused
☐ depressed
☐ ironic?

Discuss your answers in pairs and then tell the rest of the class what you thought?

Task 5 Speaker's way of talking

Why did you choose your answers to Task 4? What influenced you? Was it the:

'quality' of his voice: warm, rich, thin, cold, harsh, tense, etc.
speed: fast, slow, 'normal'
volume: loud, quiet, 'normal'
type of words used: formal, everyday, slang, mixture of types.

> **Hints on listening**
>
> There will be more work on speakers' personality and attitudes in the rest of this course. It is as important to judge these well as it is to understand the actual words used.

2

Job stereotypes

1 Pre-listening

Task 1 Reading and discussion

Read the text and discuss the questions below.

In Britain, people tend to make jokes about some jobs or professions, or to hold stereotyped views of them. For example, sailors are supposed to have a 'wife in every port', university professors are often seen as absent-minded or forgetful. Other jobs may be well-paid or very responsible, but the general public thinks they are funny or rather boring.

Even though the Equal Opportunities Commission has made some progress in Britain, some jobs are still seen as being more suitable for men, or for women.

These are all examples of prejudices or stereotypes which understandably irritate the people who have the jobs!

- Is the situation the same in your country?
- Is there a type of job that people joke about or which there is a prejudice about?

2 Listening

Task 1 Getting the main ideas

Listen to Part one of the recording in which six people talk about their jobs. Complete the table with the most important information.

	Person's job	*Prejudice about the job*
1		
2		
3		
4		
5		
6		

Compare your answers in pairs. Listen again if you want to. Check your answers with the rest of the class.

Task 2 Discussion

Did any of the prejudices about the jobs in Task 1 surprise you? What do people in your country generally think about these jobs?

Tell a partner what is the same and what is different in your country and then tell the rest of the class.

Task 3 Building a context

In any society, some jobs are well thought of and have a higher status. Others have a lower status, even though they may be better paid.

Look at the list below. Which job, in your society, would have the highest status? Which job would have the lowest status?

☐ lawyer ☐ sales representative
☐ nurse ☐ diplomat
☐ school teacher ☐ politician
☐ engineer ☐ estate agent
☐ accountant ☐ doctor

Tell the rest of the class your results.

Task 4   Note-taking at speed

Listen to Part two Section 1 of the interview and write down the names of the professions considered in the survey. There are ten names in all. Do not worry if you do not get them all the first time

. . . .

. . . .

. . . .

. . . .

. . . .

Compare your answers in pairs. Listen again if you want to. Check your answers with the rest of the class.

Task 5   Predicting information

What do you think the children thought about these jobs? Which do you think they put 'top' and which 'bottom'?

Write your predictions here. You can put one or two jobs in the 'top' section and one or two in the 'bottom' section.

Top jobs   **Bottom jobs**

. . . .

. . . .

Task 6   Listening for detail

The sociologist in the interview tells us a lot about the children's opinions of the engineering profession. Read the questionnaire they were given and then listen to Section 2 of the interview. Underline the answers that the majority of children gave. (The first example has been done for you.)

Questionnaire

The job of an engineer is:

1   clean/dirty
2   of high status/low status
3   responsible/subordinate
4   secure/insecure
5   well paid/badly paid
6   interesting/boring

An engineer is likely to be:

  7   interesting company/boring company
  8   smartly dressed/badly dressed
  9   hardworking/lazy
10   reliable/unreliable
11   friendly/unfriendly
12   cheerful/depressed

Check your answers in pairs. Listen again if you want to. Check your answers with the whole class.

Task 7   Listening for detail

Listen to Section 3 of the interview. Try to put the professions into the exact order given by the children. Put the profession with the highest status first.

High status

     1 ....

     2 ....

     3 ....

     4 ....

     5 ....

     6 ....

     7 ....

     8 ....

     9 ....

   10 ....

Low status

Compare your answers in pairs. Listen again if you want to.

Did the children put the same jobs in 'top' and 'bottom' position as you did in Task 5? Discuss your answers with the rest of the class.

3   Follow-up

Task 1   Expressing contrast

📼 Listen to Section 3 again and complete these sentences which show
ways of expressing contrast in English.

In fact 90% of the children associated him with 'dirty work' . . . .

. . . . 76% for the electrical engineer and 68% for the civil engineer.

He was the only one that the majority of children felt would be 'gloomy'

. . . . cheerful.

Listen again and see how many other expressions of contrast you can
find.

Task 2   Expressing contrast

In spoken English, we often express a contrast between two things
by stressing the words that are in contrast.

Here is an example from Unit 1. The words that are in contrast have
been joined by a line.

. . . a female who thinks she is mating with a large   warm toad may
in fact have been deceived by a small   cold one.

Look at this section of the transcript of what the sociologist said.
Join the pairs of words that are in contrast. (The first example has
been done for you.)

Section 2
. . . they also thought that the job was of 'low status' and
'subordinate' — that is the engineer is more likely to take orders
than to give them . . .

. . . the majority of children chose positive comments except that they
thought the engineer was likely to be 'badly' rather than 'well-dressed'

Section 3
. . . Funnily enough, he was the only one that the majority of children felt
would be 'gloomy' rather than 'cheerful'.

Check your answers in pairs and then with the rest of the class.

Task 3   Expressing contrast

📼 Listen to Part three of the recording which gives these extracts from
the interview again. Pay particular attention to the words that are in
contrast.

1 Pre-listening

Task 1 Building a context

These are pictures of a well-known flavouring

as it looks while it is growing and

as it looks dried and ready for sale in a market

- Do you know its name in English?
- Is it used in cooking in your country?
- How would you describe its taste?

3

Hot stuff

2   Listening

> **Hints on listening**
>
> *Coping with spontaneous speech*
>
> In this recording, a woman is telling a story spontaneously to a
> friend. When someone is speaking in a relaxed way like this,
> there is usually a lot of repetition and hesitation. Do not worry if
> you do not understand every word immediately, because the
> repetition gives you a second chance to pick up information you
> missed the first time.

Task 1   Getting the main ideas

The main points of the story are shown in the questions below. Read
them before you listen and use them to help you build up the story.

Now listen to the woman telling her story about growing her own
food and answer the questions.

1   List the plants she tried to grow.   . . . .

. . . .

. . . .

2   In which part of the house was she
    growing them?   . . . .

3   Which plants were successful?   . . . .

4   Which plants were the most
    successful?   . . . .

5   Where did the speaker get the
    most successful plants?   . . . .

. . . .

. . . .

6   How many plants of this type did
    she get?   . . . .

7   What did she do with them?   . . . .

8 Does she think she can grow them
 again? . . . .

9 Why? . . . .

. . . .

Check your answers in pairs and listen again if you want to.

Task 2   Re-telling the story

In pairs, use your answers to Task 1 to build up notes to help you tell
the story in your own words.

Re-tell the story to the rest of the class.

3   Follow-up

Task 1   Vocabulary

Listen to the woman's story again.

Collect all the words and phrases she uses to talk about success and
failure. Some examples are given.

success

managed . . . . *did OK* . . . .

. . . .

they actually were doing rather well . . . .
failure

. . . . *semi-disaster* . . . .

. . . .

. . . . *that was the end of that* . . . .

Hints on listening

Things to notice about spontaneous speech

1 Hesitation noises, e.g. *er, um*
2 Phrases used to 'fill in' while the speaker thinks of what to
  say next, e.g. *well, sort of, kind of,* you know, *I mean,* etc.

Task 2   Speaker's way of talking

📼 Look at the transcript on page 77. Listen to the recording again and follow on the transcript, noticing the hesitation noises and 'fillers'.

What hesitation noises and fillers are typical of this speaker?

Task 3   Reading and discussing

Read these two easy recipes which use the vegetable mentioned in the recording.

EGG AND TOMATO SAMBAL
(from Indonesia)

Ingredients
3 tomatoes
2 eggs
1 onion
1 chopped red pepper (chilli)
salt
pepper
oil for frying

Fry the onion until it is golden brown. Add the sliced tomatoes and the chopped chilli. Break the eggs and mix them well with the onion and chilli. Add the salt and pepper. Cook for another 3 minutes and serve.

SAUCE FOR SPAGHETTI WITH OLIVE OIL, RED PEPPER AND GARLIC
(from Italy)

Ingredients
1 chopped red pepper
2 cloves of garlic
olive oil
chopped parsley

(You can change the quantities of pepper and garlic to obtain a stronger sauce if you can bear it!)

Fry the garlic and the pepper lightly in the olive oil. Pour it all over the cooked spaghetti. Sprinkle the chopped parsley on top.

Can you think of a recipe from your country in which this vegetable is used? Explain it to the rest of the class.

1 Pre-listening

Look at this postcard. It was sent to an expert on the popular radio programme, 'Animals and Birds'.

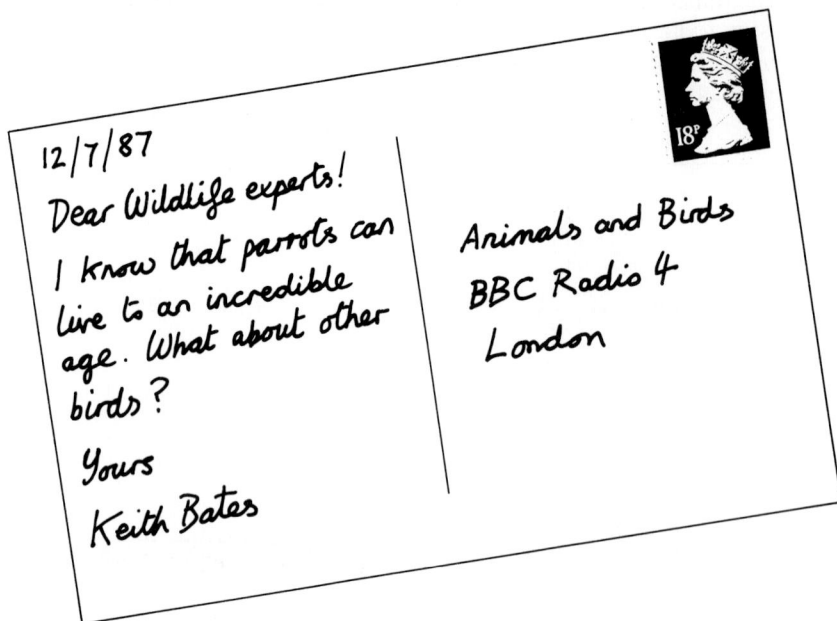

12/7/87

Dear Wildlife experts!
I know that parrots can
live to an incredible
age. What about other
birds?

Yours
Keith Bates

Animals and Birds
BBC Radio 4
London

The recording you will hear later gives the expert's reply.

2 Listening

Hints on listening

Coping with unknown words

When you are listening to spoken English you may hear words that you are unfamiliar with. You may want to look them up in a dictionary or ask someone about them later. But how are you going to remember them? Writing them down is the obvious answer.

We all know that English spelling is not very regular, so you needn't worry about getting the spelling absolutely correct. The important thing is to write down spellings that are at least reasonable, and which help you to remember the pronunciation or allow you to start a search through the dictionary.

Task 1   Mini-dictation

This task will help you gain confidence in writing down unusual words that you hear.

Look at pictures 1–6. They show six different species of bird. Listen to Part one of the recording in which someone says the English name of each type of bird. Write the correct name under each picture.

1 . . . .

2 . . . .

3 . . . .

4 . . . .

5 . . . .

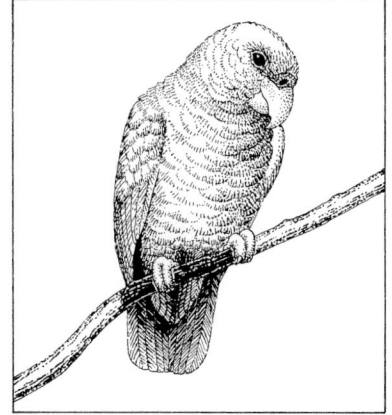

6 . . . .

Compare what you have written in pairs. Check the spellings and see if you can remember how to pronounce the words.

Your teacher will give you the correct spellings and will discuss the sounds of the words and their spellings with you.

Now you know the correct spellings, copy them (opposite the pictures) in the chart, below the heading, 'Species of bird'.

Species of bird	*Age of oldest known specimen*	*Date of death*	*Place of death*
1	74 (at least)		
2		—	UK zoo
3		—	—
4		—	—
5		—	—
6			

Task 2   Listening for detail

Listen to the extract from the radio programme in Part two of the recording and fill in the table with the information given. The first two examples are partly done for you.

Check your answers in pairs and listen again if you want to. Then check your answers with the rest of the class.

3 Follow-up

Task 1 Expressing certainty and uncertainty

When the speaker gave the information about each bird he also showed how confident he felt that what he said was accurate. Listen to the recording again and fill in the table below to show whether the speaker thinks his information is questionable, probably correct or absolutely reliable. The first example has been done for you.

Species of bird	In the speaker's opinion, the recorded age for this bird is:			Speaker's exact words
	questionable	probably correct	absolutely reliable	
1		✓		
2				
3				
4				
5				
6				

Check your answers in pairs. Listen again if you want to. Then check your answers with the rest of the class.

Task 2   Expressing certainty and uncertainty

Listen again, and write down, on the right of the table, the exact words used by the speaker to indicate his certainty about each piece of information.

If he makes no comment about his uncertainty, what does this imply?

> **Hints on listening**
>
> *Intonation*
>
> Generally, a speaker keeps his/her voice up until he/she has finished a piece of information. It is useful to be able to recognize this, so that you can avoid interrupting someone (unless you want to!).

Task 3   Recognizing intonation

Listen to the five short pieces of speech in Part 3a of the recording. Decide for each one whether the speaker has finished or not.

1 ☐ We've got coffee and tea and coca cola . . . .

2 ☐ Well the principal products are rubber and oil . . . .

3 ☐ There are useful articles on this subject by Brown Andrews Jones Smith . . . .

   . . . .

4 ☐ I suggest you read Brown and Andrews . . . .

5 ☐ The clinic is open Monday and Tuesday and Thursday . . . .

   . . . .

Listen to the sentences again in Part 3b of the recording. This time the unfinished ones have been completed. Write down the missing words. Listen again to make sure you can hear the difference between finished and unfinished pieces of information.

Task 4   Recognizing intonation

Listen to Part two of the recording again and read the transcript on page 78. Try to notice how, when the speaker keeps his voice up, he has not completed what he has to say, and when he goes down, he has finished a piece of information.

5

Home computers

1 Pre-listening

Task 1   Discussion

How do you feel about computers?

Some people hate them, other people are fascinated by them, others simply think of them as useful aids to modern living.

Choose the statements which reflect your own experience and feelings.

1   Your experience

- ☐ I use one regularly for my work.
- ☐ I have one at home.
- ☐ I have used one occasionally.
- ☐ I have no direct experience.
- ☐ I am used to receiving things like computerized bank statements and bills.

2   Your feelings

- ☐ I am scared of them.
- ☐ I think they are the key to any future progress.
- ☐ I am fascinated by them.
- ☐ I don't care about them.
- ☐ I think they can be dangerous if wrongly used.

Discuss your answers in pairs. Support your answers with reasons and details. Tell the rest of the class what you think.

2 Listening

Task 1 Prediction

Think of some reasons why an ordinary person might buy a computer to use at home. Exchange your reasons with the rest of the class.

Task 2 Getting the main ideas

Listen to Part 1 Section 1 of the story in which a woman is talking about her experiences with a home computer.

She says there are three main types of home computer user. What are they? Write them down in the table below. Put a tick against the kind of owner the speaker says she now is.

	Types of computer owner	
1		
2		
3		

Task 3 Re-telling a story

Listen to Section 1 of the story again in which the speaker describes her 'disaster', and take notes on what happened.

Use the framework below if it helps you.

1 What did she want the program to help her do?

. . . .

2 What went wrong?

. . . .

3 There was a happy end to the story. What happened?

. . . .

In pairs, expand your notes and build up the story of what happened. One or two people could try telling their version of the story to the rest of the class.

Task 4 Listening for detail

In Section 2 the speaker mentions the titles of three computer programmes which she bought ready-made. What are they? What does each program do? Fill in the table on the next page as you listen.

	Program title	*What the program does*
1		
2		
3		

3 Follow-up

Task 1 Speaker's way of talking

How would you describe the way in which the speaker presented her story?

Choose one or more of these adjectives and add any of your own:

light-hearted	serious	. . . .
ironical	humorous	. . . .
hysterical	nervous	. . . .
irritated	resentful	. . . .
angry	bored	. . . .

What clues did you use to help you decide? (Look back at the Follow-up tasks in Unit 1.) Discuss your ideas with the rest of the class.

Task 2 Speaker's way of talking

Now listen to Part two in which another person tells the same story.

Which version of the story was told by the person who *actually* had the experience?

Which speaker did you find easier to understand? Why do you think this was?

☐ speed of speaking   ☐ amount of repetition
☐ accent   ☐ number of other speakers

Discuss your ideas with the rest of the class. Suggest any other reasons that are not mentioned above.

1 Pre-listening

Task 1 Vocabulary

Complete this list of the 'five senses' in English.

sight
smell

. . . .

. . . .

. . . .

Check your list with other people in the class.

Task 2 Vocabulary

Look at the words below. They are all connected with listening, hearing and difficulties with hearing. How many do you already know? Use a dictionary to find the meanings of any you do not know.

nouns	verbs	descriptive phrases/adjectives
perception	to amplify	ambiguous
vowel	to perceive	hard-of-hearing
consonant		hearing impaired
lip-reading		auditory
stress		deaf
pitch		
rhythm		
vibration		

In pairs, practise asking for, and giving meanings like this:

A *Can you explain* | *lip-reading* | *please?*
   What does | | *mean, please?*

B *Yes, it means* | . . .
   It means |

Task 3 Reading and discussion

Read the passage and stop to answer each set of questions.

LIP-READING

One of the basic skills that has helped many deaf and hard-of-hearing people is lip-reading, which means guessing from the shape and movement of a person's lips what he or she could be saying.

Many hearing people have this skill to some extent in their native language. Simple messages can often be passed by this means in noisy surroundings, or from the other side of a glass partition, but many deaf people have developed this skill to a very high degree.

6

Glasses that hear

How skilled are you at lip-reading in English?

Look at these photographs. They show different moments in the girl's reply to the question, 'Can you come round tonight?'.

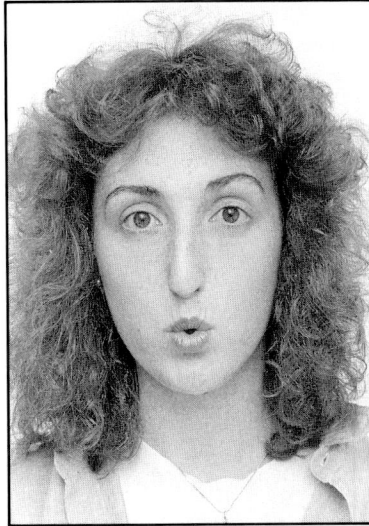

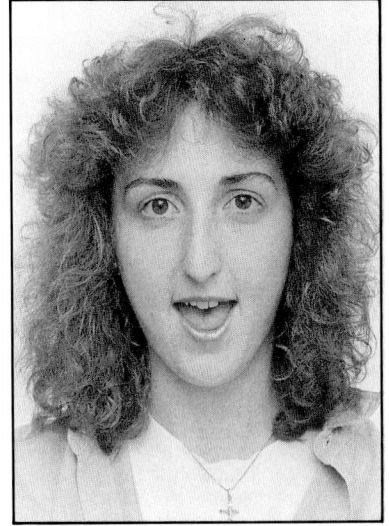

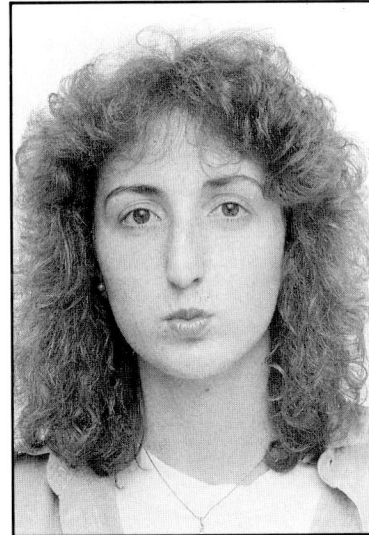

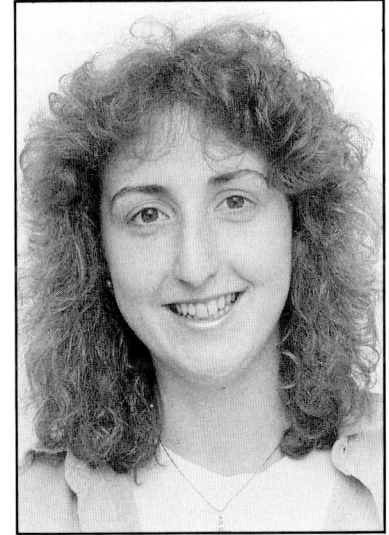

Look at the shape of her lips and decide which of the three possible replies she is giving.

1 Sorry, I'm busy.
2 Ooh, yes please.
3 What time?

Discuss your answer in pairs and check your decision with the rest of the class.

Now try saying some simple phrases in English to your partner —
but without making any sound! See if your partner can understand
you.

PROBLEMS WITH LIP-READING

However skilled a person may be at lip-reading, there can still be
problems. You probably noticed in the previous exercises that many
sounds are made with the same lip positions. This can make the message
ambiguous or unclear. Of course, using the context — what you have
already understood, what you know about the topic, etc. — you can
resolve many ambiguities, but context is not always enough.

A hearing person uses many clues to help him or her understand a
person's attitude or mood, the pitch of the voice, for example, or its
volume. These are not things that most deaf people can use to help
them. They can use the facial expression, yes, but not even this is always
clear in its message. Look at these photographs, for example:

What emotion do you think the person is showing in each one?
Tell the rest of the class what you think.

2   Listening

Task 1   Getting the main ideas

Listen to the interview which tells you about some new devices that
could help deaf and hard-of-hearing people overcome some of the
problems mentioned in the reading passage.

Listen to the whole interview once and write the names of the four
devices mentioned in the table on page 28. Don't fill in column 2 yet.
You will do this in Task 2.

Check your answer in pairs and discuss any differences in spelling.
(Remember, provided you have written down a reasonable version of
the word, you need not worry if your spelling is not exact at this
stage.)

Task 2   Getting the main ideas

Listen again and complete the chart with notes on how each device
helps deaf people. Some of the information is already included in the
chart.

	Name of the device	*What it does*
1		
2	Mini-fonator	
3		messages tapped out at one end using push-button phone, appear on a screen at other end.
4	Telesign	

3   Follow-up

> **Hints on listening**
>
> *Coping with unstressed words*
>
> Many learners of English find it very difficult to hear unstressed words. They seem very unclear to them. You need to use the context and your knowledge of English grammar to help you.

Task 1   Hearing exactly what the speaker said

Look at this extract from the transcript. Before you listen again, try to fill in the gaps with words you think make sense.

This week we are looking . . . . ways in which deaf . . . .

hard-of-hearing people . . . . be helped to make . . . . most

of the skills they already have in order . . . . communicate more

easily . . . . other people.

Check your answers in pairs and then listen again and check your answers from the recording. The missing words were all unstressed on the tape. Did the work you did before listening again prepare you to 'hear' them more easily?

7

A post-industrial industry

1 Pre-listening

Task 1 Building a context

Do you recognize this tree? What does it produce? (A hint: it represents a very large proportion of Malaysia's Gross National Product.)

Think of some of the things in whose manufacture it is used. Write down at least three of them. Tell the rest of the class your suggestions. Your teacher will put them all on the board.

You can now see why this product is so important strategically. It is also important because it is a natural product, which is produced without using fuels such as oil or coal. You will hear more about this in the taped discussion.

2   Listening

Task 1   Predicting language

This exercise is to help you 'hear' more easily some of the weakly-pronounced words in the passage. Use your knowledge of English grammar to help you fill in the gaps in this extract from the passage.

Most manufacturing industries . . . . based on fossil fuels — coal

. . . . oil. Now the problem . . . . that these . . . . not

last for ever. They . . . . finite. Sooner . . . . later they

. . . . run out. Now rubber is . . . . natural product.

. . . . only energy source involved . . . . its creation is

sunlight. Now sunlight we hope . . . . outlast coal . . . . oil.

Sunlight . . . . free, so . . . . is much cheaper . . . .

produce natural rubber . . .

Check your answers in pairs and then with the rest of the class.

Task 2   Predicting information

Now you know something about the subject of the discussion. What other aspects of it do you think will be covered in the recording? Choose as many of the ideas below as you think are likely.

☐   a list of other countries where rubber is important
☐   a discussion of how rubber is produced in Malaysia
☐   a discussion of economic and social problems in Malaysia
☐   a discussion of the problems with fossil fuels

Compare your answers in pairs.

Task 3   Getting the main ideas

You are going to hear a discussion between two experts. It is about a situation, a number of problems, and their possible solutions.

Look at the chart on page 32 carefully before you start to listen, and make sure that you understand it.

Listen to Part one of the discussion and fill in the chart with the important information under each heading.

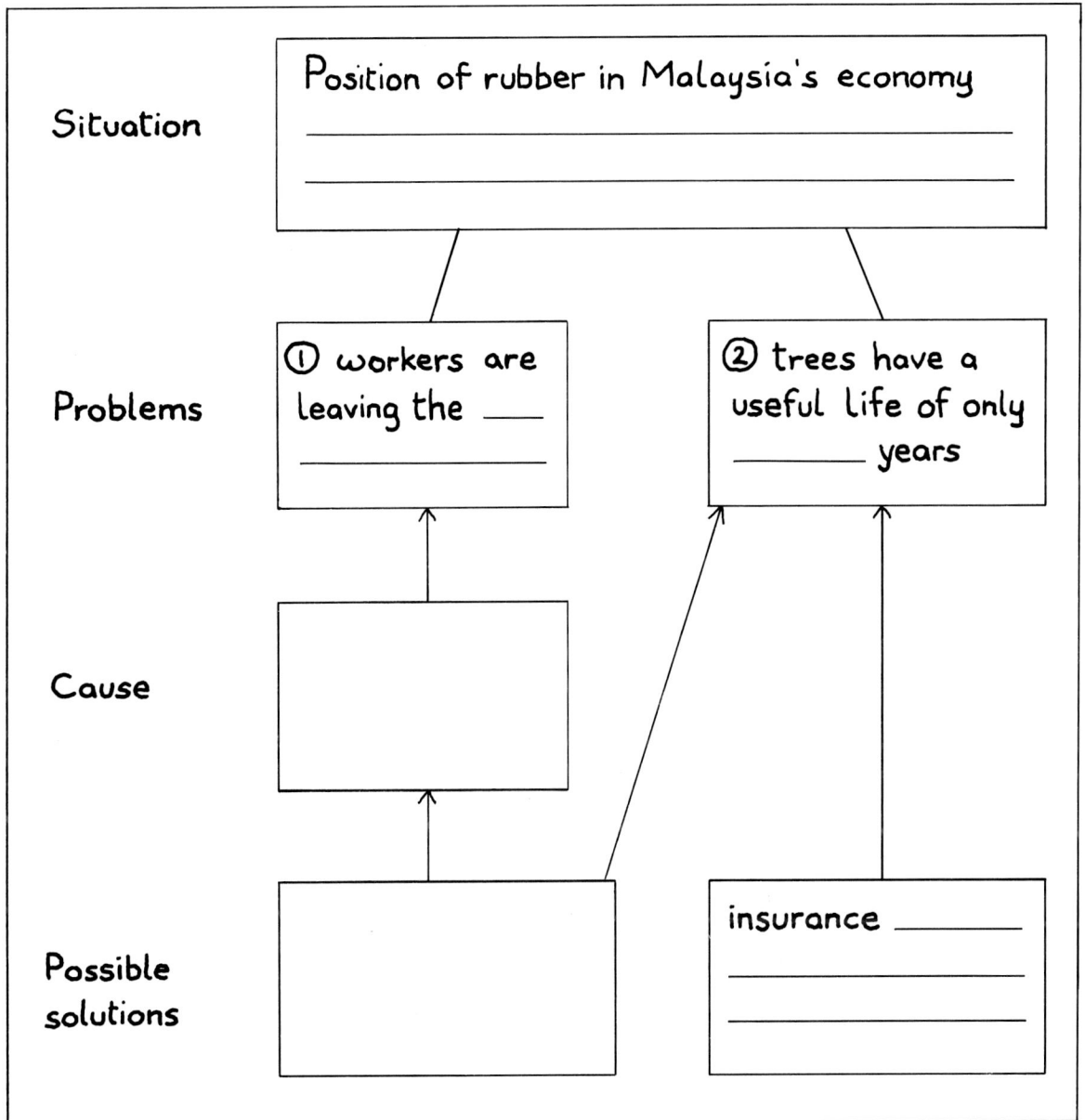

Situation	**Position of rubber in Malaysia's economy**
Problems	① workers are leaving the ____ _____
	② trees have a useful life of only _____ years
Cause	
Possible solutions	
	insurance _____

Task 4   Recognizing tone and attitude

Listen to Part one of the discussion again. There are three speakers: the Chairperson (a woman) and two 'experts' (both men), Andrew Frobisher and Dr Harry Benson.

Which of the adjectives opposite describe the attitudes and emotions of each of the speakers? Add any more that you think would be appropriate.

	Chairperson	Mr Frobisher	Dr Benson
nervous			
self-satisfied			
scornful			
irritated			
pompous			
confident			
annoyed			
resentful			
amused			
worried			
passionate			
nostalgic			
relieved			

Compare your answers in pairs and with the rest of the class.

Try to decide at what points in the discussion the speakers showed the different attitudes and emotions. Listen again to confirm your ideas.

Task 5   Listening for detail

Read these sentences below and on page 34, then listen to Part one of the discussion again and fill in the gaps with the detailed information.

1   Rubber represents approximately .... % of Malaysia's Gross National Product.

2   Each rubber tree is tapped by hand .... day.

3   One worker is capable of looking after a total of . . . . trees.

4   A rubber tree's useful life is about . . . . years.

5   The number of Malaysians working directly with rubber in 1981 was . . . .

Task 6   Getting the main ideas

Now listen to part two of the discussion. Dr Benson discussed diversification on rubber plantations by raising livestock.

He shows the audience an OHP (overhead projection). Fill in his OHP with the correct information.

Ways of diversifying economy

Livestock

	Type of animal	Successful	Reasons
1			
2			
3			

3 Follow-up

Think about the whole discussion — Parts one and two — and try
these exercises.

Task 1 Detecting hostility

Dr Benson and Mr Frobisher were clearly not very fond of each
other! Listen again and collect examples of how they showed it. The
table below may help you.

	by Dr Benson	*by Mr Frobisher*
Interruption		
Nasty comments		
Other		

Task 2 Judging performance

Which of the two experts did you like more? Or did you find them
equally impossible? Would this type of behaviour occur in a public
discussion in your country? How would speakers have shown
hostility in your country?

Did you think the Chairperson was:

effective
too weak
simply facing an impossible situation?

Tell the rest of the class what you think.

Task 3 Dictation

Do you think that the prediction task on page 31 helped you to 'hear'
the unstressed words better?

If you have a language laboratory or your own cassette-recorder
available, choose a very short section of the recording (not more than
30 seconds) and listen to it, using the 'pause' and 'stop' buttons. Try
to write down the speaker's actual words. When you are satisfied,
check what you have written against the actual transcript on page 82.

Did you leave out any words because you did not hear them? Play the
tape again and follow the words on the transcript.

8

Bottoms up!

1 Pre-listening

Task 1 Discussion

Discuss these questions with the whole class.

- Do you recognize this place?
- What do you think the people are doing?
- If you had seen them would you have tried to find out what was going on?
- If so, how would you have done it:
  by asking them directly?
  by going closer and watching?

2 Listening

> **Hints on listening**
>
> *Coping with spontaneous speech*
>
> You are going to hear a story told spontaneously, and as is usual in these cases, there is much less 'real' information than you would expect to find in a lecture or informal talk. The speaker makes a few main points, but concentrates on the effect she is making, often repeating herself for emphasis and adding new details gradually. You don't find out the answer to the mystery until the end of the story.

Task 1   Getting the main ideas and some connected details

Listen to the woman telling her story about what she saw and what she found out.

Fill in as much of the chart as you can. Do not expect to get all the details the first time you hear the story. Concentrate on getting the main points first and then the details. Listen straight through, as often as you need.

	Country	*City*	*Specific place*	*Other details*
1 WHERE the incident happened:				

	Day	*Time*
2 WHEN the incident happened:		

	How many people?	*Their relationship*	*What exactly were they doing?*
3 WHO the speaker saw:			

Task 2   Listening for more detail

Listen again and concentrate on information about the plant the people were picking.

How does the speaker describe it in terms of:

habits and habitat . . . .

smell . . . .

taste . . . .

use in cookery . . . .

how it is prepared for use in cookery? . . . .

3   Follow-up

Task 1   Discussion

Here are some pictures of what the people wanted

in their natural form

as you use them in cooking

Discuss the following questions with the rest of the class.

- Have you ever tried them?
- Do you like them?
- How would you describe their taste?
- Are they used in any dishes in your country?

Task 2   Speaker's way of talking

Listen to the story again.

What impression do you get of the speaker as she tells her story? Is she:

relaxed
tense
excited
trying to amuse
trying to impress
serious
sad?

Can you think of any other ways to describe her mood or intentions. Does her way of speaking change during the story?

Listen to the recording once more with these questions in mind then tell the rest of the class what you think.

Task 3   Noticing what happens in spontaneous speech

Listen again with the transcript on page 83 and collect some more examples of what happens in spontaneous speech.

Do you remember if any part of the story was difficult for you to understand when you first heard it, because of any of these features?

Did any of these features help you to understand the story?

Task 4   Thinking about your own language

What is the typical 'hesitation noise' people make when speaking in your language? Demonstrate it to the rest of the class.

Are there any phrases which people use like the English 'sort of' and 'I mean' to gain time when they are thinking? Say one or two of these phrases to the rest of the class and give the translation in English.

Many English speakers hesitate a lot when speaking spontaneously. This is considered quite acceptable. Are people in your country criticized if they hesitate a lot when they speak?

9

Art or technology?

1 Pre-listening

Task 1 Vocabulary

What do you think the photograph shows?

If you are not sure, look at the words below. They are all connected with the topic.

nouns	verbs	adjectives
curd	ferment	spicy
whey	ripen	sharp
flavour	coagulate	pungent
bacteria	pasteurise	mild

In pairs, discuss the list and try to agree on what the topic is. Use a dictionary to check the meaning of the words you are not sure of.

2 Listening

Task 1 Predicting language

Now that you know the general topic, suggest other words you would expect to hear in a talk on the subject. Try to think of at least five and write them here.

. . . .

. . . .

. . . .

In pairs, compare your words and then tell them to the rest of the class. Your teacher will write them all up on the board.

Task 2   Getting the main information

Listen to the talk which gives a history of this process from its origins
until fairly recent times. Fill in the boxes with the relevant
information.

1   The date and place of origin

2   The name of the people who
    developed and spread the
    process

3   The dates when this happened

4   The word in their language
    that is the origin of the English
    word 'cheese'

5   The major technological
    development at the end of the
    19th century

In pairs, check your answers and listen again if necessary.

3   Follow-up

Task 1   Discussion

Discuss the following questions with the whole class.

- What is the word for cheese in your language?
- Is it similar or different to the English word 'cheese'?
- If it is similar, do you think the words are related?
- Is your word related to a word in any other language?

Task 2   Vocabulary

Is there a special cheese typical of your country?

If so, write down its name here. . . . .

Look at this list of adjectives. Underline the ones you could use to describe the cheese's characteristics.

flavour

sweet	pungent	mild	sharp
bitter	fruity	strong	rancid-tasting
spicy			

texture

smooth	soft	hard	grainy
rubbery	crumbly	dry	

other characteristics

long-lasting   smelly   with air bubbles
with streaks of mould

source

cow's milk   goat's milk   sheep's milk
the milk of some other animal (say which)

Task 3   Describing

Use the words you have underlined to help you describe your cheese to the rest of the class. Use this outline:

One type of cheese we have in my country is called . . . .

It is made of . . . .*'s milk and has a* . . . .

. . . . *taste. Its texture is* . . . . . .

. . . .

Then you can mention any other characteristics it has, and any special uses it has in cooking.

Task 4   Writing a summary

Listen to the recording again, and take more notes if you wish. Now write a short summary of the history of cheese-making in your own words.

1 Pre-listening

Task 1 Discussion

Discuss these questions with the rest of the class.

1 What is the most peculiar type of food that you have ever tried? For example has anyone eaten durian, snails, etc.

10

How disgusting!

2 What effect did it have on you:

- ☐ nauseating
- ☐ exciting
- ☐ worrying
- ☐ satisfying
- ☐ not much effect at all?

2 Listening

Task 1 Identifying the speakers

Listen to some people talking about the exotic cheeses they have tried.

How many different speakers can you identify?

- ☐ two
- ☐ three
- ☐ four
- ☐ five

Task 2   Recognizing tone and intention

Do you think these people are trying to:

☐ inform one another
☐ amuse one another
☐ compete with one another.

(You can choose more than one.)

In pairs, check your answers and then tell them to the rest of the class. Justify your answers with clues from the language the speakers used — their tone of voice, the words they used, etc.

Task 3   Listening for detail

Listen again and fill in the chart with information about the different types of cheese the speakers mention.

Type of cheese (from what animal)	Characteristics	Country of origin
1 Cat	—	—
2 guinea pig	—	—
3		
4		
5		

3   Follow-up

Task 1   Ways of capturing attention

The speakers were having a friendly conversation, but each one was trying to tell a better story than the others. This meant there was a lot of interruption and a lot of language used to capture the attention of the other speakers.

Listen again and try to fill in the gaps in the extracts from the transcript with the words used to capture the attention of the other speakers.

1 **Woman** . . . they just wanted to know about the composition of

their milk.

Older man . . . . I've tried llama's cheese.

2 **Woman** . . . . what I really

like is that Greek goat's cheese . . .

3 **Woman** . . . . I think the most peculiar cheese I ever had

was in Sardinia.

Task 2 Reading with rhythm

Little Miss Muffet
Sat on a tuffet
Eating her curds and whey
There came a big spider
That sat down beside her
And frightened Miss Muffet away.

Try reading the rhyme in unison with the recording. The stresses are marked to help you. This type of speaking practice will help you with your listening since it will make you notice how native speakers pronounce the unstressed syllables when they speak quickly.

11

My computer makes me sick!

1 Pre-listening

Task 1 Collecting information

Do you remember what the speaker in Unit 5 said about the supposed dangers of working for too long with computers? Write down what you remember.

. . . .

. . . .

Check your memory with the rest of the class.

Listen again to Unit 5 if you want to refresh your memory.

2 Listening

Task 1 Predicting information

You are going to hear part of a radio talk about the dangers of computer use. What hazards do you think the speaker will emphasize? Make a guess and write down your ideas.

. . . .

. . . .

. . . .

. . . .

Tell the rest of the class what you think.

Task 2 Getting the main information

Listen to Part one of the talk once through and write down all the health hazards the speaker mentions.

. . . .

. . . .

. . . .

. . . .

Compare your answers with the list of predictions you made. Are there any new things? Did you predict anything you did not hear on the recording?

Listen again to make sure you have collected all the hazards the speaker mentions.

In pairs, compare your answers and listen again if you need to resolve any differences.

Task 3   Listening for detail

The speaker divides the hazards into two types. Write these as headings in the table and put the hazards under the appropriate heading.

Hazards	
1	2 . . . .

Discuss your answers in pairs.

Task 4   Listening for more detail

The speaker describes surveys which have been conducted on professional and amateur users of computers. Complete the diagram on the next page with hazards which are a particular threat to professionals, to amateurs, or which are common to both.

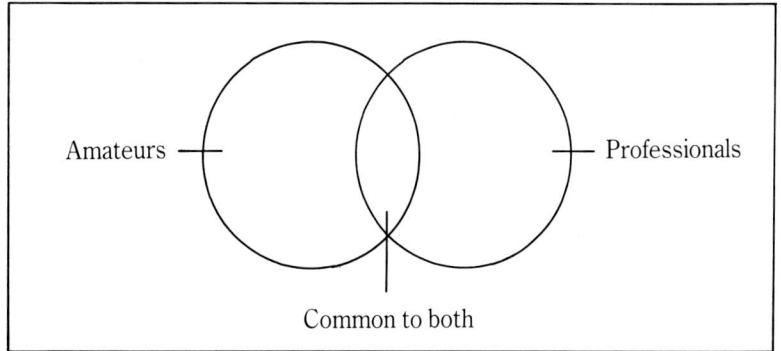

Which group, professional or amateur does the speaker think is in

more danger? Why is this? . . . .

. . . .

Task 5   Prediction

What precautions or remedies do you think would be useful to use
against the hazards mentioned in Part one?

What advice would you give to a frequent computer user? Write
down some of your ideas.

. . . .

. . . .

. . . .

. . . .

. . . .

Now discuss them with a partner.

Task 6   Listening for detail

Now listen to Part two of the talk in which the speaker gives advice
to people who use computers a lot. He makes five main points. Take
notes on what he says for each of them. Some of the key words are
given to help you.

Precautions to take when using a computer for long periods

---

1   light

2   eyes

3   tuning in the screen

4   position

5   exercise

Task 7   Checking your predictions

How did the advice you decided to give compare with the advice the
speaker gave?

Tell the rest of the class any ideas you had that the speaker did not
mention, and any ideas that you shared.

3 Follow-up

Task 1 Specialized vocabulary

In this unit you heard about office workers who spend many hours in front of a video terminal. One of the jobs they are often involved in is word processing, which you heard about in Unit 5.

Look at the picture of a computer and of the document that the operator is working on. Label it using words from the list below.

words you have already met:

screen	margin	heading
keyboard	line	word
paragraph	printer	letter

new words:

monitor
cable

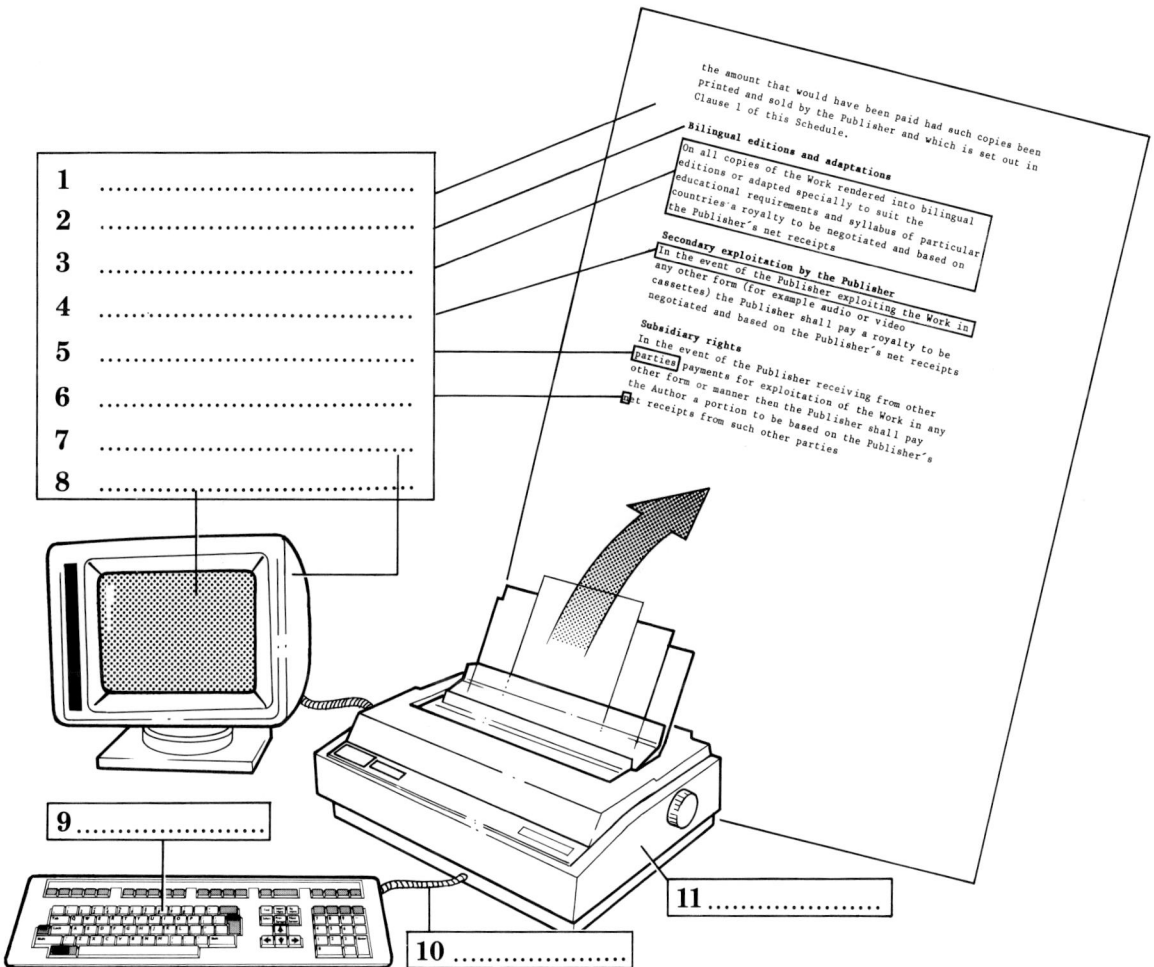

1   Pre-listening

Task 1   Vocabulary and discussion

Look at these pictures.

12
Mummy dust

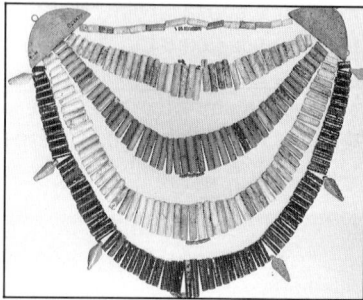

In pairs, try to label them. Tell the rest of the class which words you used.

What great civilization are the pictures connected with? Tell the rest of the class anything you know about these people.

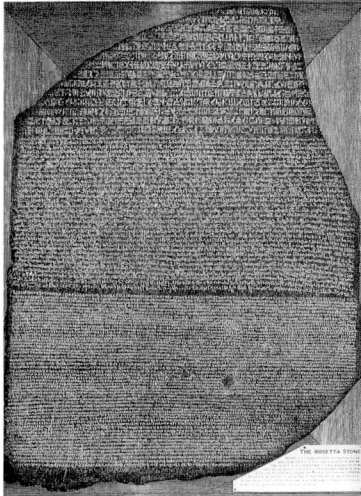

THE ROSETTA STONE

Task 2   Reading

Read the text below.

In 1799 this stone, with the same inscription in three languages was found on the western mouth of the Nile. The Rosetta Stone, now in the British Museum, is one of the sights that visitors to Britain flock to see. Before its discovery the Egyptian writing known as hieroglyphic had been a mystery to scholars. But now, since one of the languages on the stone was Greek, it was possible to decipher the other two. With this major discovery — which however took many years — public interest in Ancient Egypt reached fever pitch.

This is just one example of a series of fashions for Ancient Egypt that discoveries in archaeology have aroused over the past two centuries. The discovery of the fabulous treasure of the boy-king Tutankhamun in 1921 was another one. By then the film-making industry was well-developed and the subject of Ancient Egypt — land of mystery and magic — was irresistible to film makers and public alike. The picture given of this world may be distorted and terribly inaccurate, but the popularity and imaginative appeal of films featuring Ancient Egypt continue to this day. There is a sub-genre too, films in which a modern-day archaeological discovery is the starting-point for horrific or supernatural events, usually involving a mummy coming to life again, or a curse which follows the members of an archaeological expedition. Titles such as 'The Pharoah's Curse' or 'The Living Mummy' are typical of this genre.

The theme of the curse is very widespread, perhaps because it is popularly believed that there was a curse upon all the members of the real-life expedition which found the secret tomb of Tutankhamun — in fact many of them did die in mysterious circumstances.

Another more recent source of interest in the magical side of the Ancient Egyptians was the fashion for mysticism and paranormal phenomena in the 1960s and 1970s. During this time a lot of interest was focused on the pyramid. What most people had thought of as simply a grandiose and massive monument to a dead king or other person of importance was revealed to have strange powers.

Some people swore that a razor blade kept under a small model of a pyramid would remain almost permanently sharp. Others claimed that plants put inside a pyramid-shaped frame grew more vigorously. You could buy small pyramids 'for home use' in many shops. Some people even erected a pyramid over their bed and said they slept better and felt more healthy generally. No one has ever quite explained these phenomena, or worked out if the Egyptians attributed similar powers to their own pyramids, but anyway the fashion seems, like so many, to have passed.

The passages you are going to hear are about more scientific types of interest in Ancient Egypt, but even these are often inspired by the imaginative hold this marvellous civilization has over many people.

Task 3　Getting the main ideas

According to the reading text, Ancient Egypt has interested the general public in several main ways since the discovery of the Rosetta Stone. Complete the table to show what these ways were.

Type of interest	√
1　Interest in the language	

Task 4

Opposite each entry in the table above, indicate whether this aspect of Ancient Egypt caused any interest in your country.

Tell the rest of the class what aspects of Ancient Egypt are best known in your country.

2　Listening

This unit and the next two contain a radio interview in which an expert talks about modern discoveries about the ancient Egyptians.

In this unit you will hear the presenter of the programme talking about some of the types of people who have been interested in ancient Egypt, and about some of the topics that are of particular interest in the study of ancient Egypt.

Task 1   Getting the main ideas

📻 Read the list of topics and types of people. Listen to the recording and tick the ones that the presenter mentions.

Topics   **People**
☐ architecture   ☐ novelists
☐ magic   ☐ fashion designers
☐ astronomy   ☐ artists
☐ art   ☐ archaeologists
☐ mummification   ☐ anthropologists
☐ medicine   ☐ film-makers
☐ religion   ☐ doctors
☐ literature

Task 2   Listening for specific information

📻 Listen to the presenter again and take notes to help you answer these questions about 'mummy dust'.

● What was it used for?

....

● Why were false mummies made?

....

● When did the black market in mummies start?

....

Task 3   Discussion and summary writing

In pairs, discuss your notes and prepare a short written summary of the story of mummy dust.

Task 4   Getting the most important theme

The presenter makes a strong contrast between the attitude of people in the past to mummies and that of most modern-day scientists.

📻 Listen again and take notes on the difference in attitude.

In the past	*In the present day*

Try to express the difference in your own words to a partner and then to the rest of the class.

Task 5   Listening for more detail

You have heard about the ethical and practical reasons why modern scientists are very careful about how they treat mummies. Listen again and try to complete the detailed notes in the table.

	Ethical	*Practical*
Reasons why scientists are careful		
Ways in which they show their care		

Compare your notes in pairs. Listen again if you want to and then check your notes with the rest of the class.

3 Follow-up

Task 1 Discussion

Do you think the scientists are right to be so careful, or do you think they are being over-scrupulous?

Task 2 Predicting information

What sort of things do you think can be found out from autopsies on mummies? Make a list.

. . . .

. . . .

. . . .

Discuss your ideas with the rest of the class.

The recordings in the next two units will give you more information on this.

1 Pre-listening

Task 1 Collecting information

In Unit 12 you thought about the types of information scientists could get from the investigation of Egyptian mummies. Summarize them again on the board.

Task 2 Predicting information

Two types of professional would obviously be interested in the scientific studies of mummies — archaeologists and anthropologists. What other types of people could be usefully involved in such a study?

Choose from these and add any suggestions of your own.

- [ ] radiologists
- [ ] doctors
- [ ] physicists

- [ ] engineers
- [ ] dentists
- [ ] opticians

. . . .

. . . .

Discuss your ideas with the rest of the class.

Task 3 Talking about time

Look at the time chart on page 58. It shows the main periods of Ancient Egyptian civilization. The dates are given according to the Western BC/AD system.

- What do BC and AD stand for?
- How many years ago was:
       55 BC
       1200 BC
       300 AD?

- Try saying these dates out loud to a partner.
     3100 BC   40 AD   2130 BC   945 BC   35 AD   984 BC.

The reigns of Egyptian kings are divided into Dynasties — the first Dynasty, the twenty-third Dynasty, etc. In writing, these are usually numbered using Roman numerals. You will find it useful to be familiar with how these work.

V	= 5 or 5th	XX	= 20 or 20th
VI	= 6 or 6th	XXIX	= 29 or 29th
X	= 10 or 10th	L	= 50 or 50th
IX	= 9 or 9th	C	= 100 or 100th
		D	= 500 or 500th
		M	= 1,000 or 1,000th

13

Scientific studies

THE DYNASTIES OF EGYPT

with approximate dates

ARCHAIC
Dynasties I and II

OLD KINGDOM

Dynasty III

Dynasty IV
c. 2620 BC
Snofru
Cheops
Dedefre
Chephren
Mycerinus

Dynasty V
c. 2480 BC
Unis (the last king)

Dynasty VI
c. 2340 BC
Teti I
Pepi I
Meryre
Pepi II

FIRST INTERMEDIATE

Dynasties VII and VIII

Dynasties IX and X

MIDDLE KINGDOM

Dynasty XI

Dynasty XII
c. 2212 BC
Amenemnes I
Sesostris I
Amenemnes II
Sesostris II
Sesostris III
Amenemnes III
Sebeknofru

SECOND
INTERMEDIATE

Dynasties XIII-XVII
(including the Hyksos)

NEW KINGDOM

Dynasty XVIII
Ahmose
1575-1550 BC
Amenhotep I
1550-1528 BC
Thutmose I
1528-1510 BC
Thutmose II
1510-1490 BC
Hatshepsut
1490-1468 BC
Thutmose III
1468-1436 BC
Amenhotep II
1436-1413 BC
Thutmose IV
1413-1405 BC
Amenhotep III
1405-1367 BC
Amenhotep IV
(Akhenaten)
1367-1350 BC
Smenkhare
1350-1347 BC
Tutankhamun
1347-1339 BC
Ay
1339-1335 BC
Haremhab
1335-1308 BC

Dynasty XIX
Rameses I
1308 BC
Seti I
1309-1291 BC
Rameses II
1290-1224 BC
Merenptah
1224-1214
Amenemses
Siptah
1208-1202 BC
Seti II
Interim anarchy,
ending with a Syrian
usurper called Arsu

Dynasty XX
Setnakhte
1184-1182 BC
Rameses III
1182-1151 BC
Rameses IV
1151-1145 BC
Rameses V-XII

LATE NEW KINGDOM

Dynasty XXI
c. 1087-945 BC
Including:
Smendes
Psusennes
c. 1055

Dynasty XXII
(Libyans)
c. 945-730
Sheshonk I
Osorkon I

Takelot I
Osorkon II
Sheshonk II
Takelot II
Sheshonk III
Pemu
Sheshonk IV

Dynasty XXIII
(Libyans)
c. 817?-730 BC

Dynasty XXIV
(Ethiopians)
c. 720-715 BC

Dynasty XXV
(Ethiopians)
Including:
Piankhy
751-730 BC

SAITE

Dynasty XXVI
Psammetichus I
664-610 BC
Neko
610-595 BC
Psammeticus II
595-589 BC
Apries
589-570 BC
Amasis
570-526 BC
Psammetichus III
526-525 BC

LATE

Dynasties XXVII-XXXI

What do you think these numbers are?

IV   XXI   CCIX   XL   LXXX   XC

Say these modern dates quickly in English

1841   1953   1976   1871   1799   1921

Do you know these expressions for general periods of time?

the nineteenth century, the twentieth century
the last decade of the nineteenth century
the nineteen thirties
the early 1960s, the late seventies.

2 Listening

Task 1 Listening for detail

In Pre-listening Task 2 you predicted some of the types of professional people who might be involved in a scientific investigation of a mummy. Listen to the interview once through and write down all the professions which are mentioned.

. . . .

. . . .

. . . .

. . . .

Task 2 Listening for the main information

Listen again and complete the table to give information about the three studies discussed in detail in the interview.

	City	*Date*	*Mummy studied (name, date, etc.)*
1			—
2			—
3	Paris		

Compare your notes in pairs and listen again if you want to.
Check your notes with the rest of the class.

Task 3   Listening for more detail

Listen again and complete the table to show the three main areas of study and the detailed information which was sought for each one.

	Main area of study	*Detailed information sought*
1	medical condition	
2		height,
3		

Compare your notes in pairs and listen again if you want to.
Check your notes with the rest of the class.

3   Follow-up

Task 1   Integrating listening with reading

Look again at the time chart and find the name of the Pharaoh mentioned in the interview.

- What were his dates?
- How many years did he live?
- How long did he reign?

1 Pre-listening

Task 1 Reading

Read this text.

The Pharaoh whose mummy was studied in Paris was not just *anybody*. He was in fact one of the most remarkable and famous of all the Egyptian kings.

Here is his portrait as a young man in a statue you can see today in the British Museum.

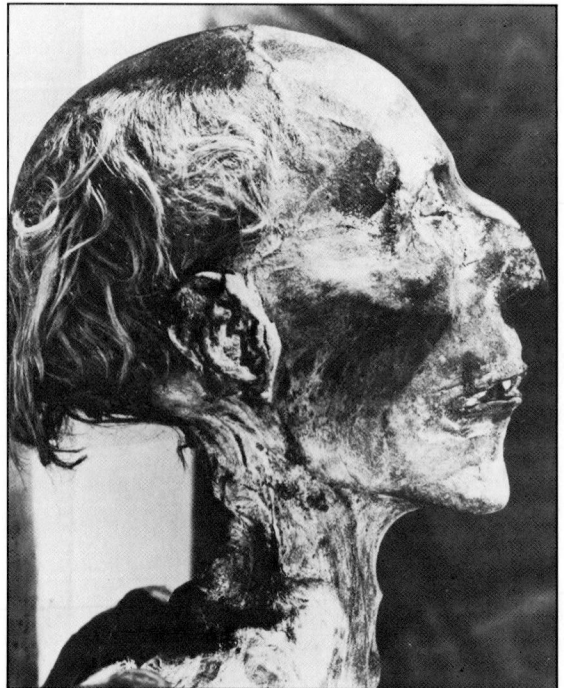

Here is his actual face — that of the mummy kept in the Cairo museum. He died old as you can see but after a long and successful reign.

Here are some facts we know about him.

He built the temple of Abu Simbel.

He was a great warrior and extended the empire of Egypt during his reign.

He is thought to be the Pharoah mentioned in the Bible at the time of Moses.

Hieroglyphics of his name look like this:

Task 2   Discussion

How do you feel when you see a real person like this on show in a museum?

Tick any of the answers that are true for you and add any other answers you want to.

☐ **1** I don't regard what I see as a real person — just a thing.
☐ **2** I find it rather disgusting.
☐ **3** It has a morbid fascination for me.
☐ **4** I think museums should show more respect — people's bodies should not be put on public display.
☐ **5** If the display can teach us something interesting I think it is all right.

6 . . . .

. . . .

Compare your answers in pairs. Tell the rest of the class what you thought.

2 Listening

This part of the interview covers two main topics:

1 What all the studies found out in general about the ancient Egyptians.
2 Particular details about Rameses II.

Task 1 Listening for detail

Listen to the interview and fill in the table with notes about the detailed discoveries made in each area of study. Concentrate on the general information but you can include information about Rameses II as well, if it is relevant.

	Main area of study	*What they found out*
1		
2		
3		

Compare your notes in pairs. Does your partner have any details that you missed, or do you disagree about anything? Listen again if you want to then check your notes with the rest of the class.

Task 2 Bringing the information together

Information about Rameses is scattered throughout the interview. Try to bring it together to make a coherent narrative of what happened during his life and after his death.

Use the note-taking framework to help you. You may remember some information about him from Unit 13, so read through the framework and see if you can fill in some of the details with information you already are sure of.

RAMESES II

1   dates of his reign: . . . .

2   age at death: . . . .

3   medical condition at
    time of death: . . . .

4   details of his
    mummification: . . . .

                         . . . .

5   where the
    archaeologists found
    him: . . . .

6   possible explanation of
    where he was found: . . . .

7   what happened in 1871: . . . .

8   what happened to his
    body in the museum: . . . .

9   what happened in 1976: . . . .

10 the condition in which
    his body is now kept: . . . .

Compare your notes in pairs. Do not look at your partner's notes but listen to what he or she says.

🎬 Listen to the interview again for any points you may have missed the first time and to resolve any disagreements.

3   Follow-up

Task 1   Re-telling the story

In pairs, reconstruct the story of 'The adventures of the body of Rameses II'.

Tell your version to the rest of the class.

Task 2   Using the passive

Because the speakers are not interested in telling the listener exactly *who* did all these things to Rameses II (in most cases nobody knows anyway), the passive structure is very frequent in this interview.

e.g.   'Although some very old individuals *were encountered* . . .'
'. . . some modern disorders *have* so far *not been found*'
'You said the body *was made up*? You mean its face *was painted*?'

Listen again and collect at least five more examples of the passive. Tell the rest of the class your examples.

Look at the transcript of the interview on page 87 to check your answers. All examples of the passive are printed in italic type.

Task 3   Remembering and re-telling

Can anyone remember the story about the discovery of 'tobacco' in Rameses' sarcophagus? Try telling it to the rest of the class.

Task 4   Reading with rhythm

Try reading the poem in unison with the recording. The stresses are marked to help you.

OZYMANDIAS OF EGYPT

I met a traveller from an antique land
Who said: Two vast and trunkless legs of stone
Stand in the desert. Near them on the sand,
Half sunk, a shatter'd visage lies, whose frown
And wrinkled lip and sneer of cold command
Tell that its sculptor well those passions read
Which yet survive, stamped on these lifeless things,
The hand that mock'd them and the heart that fed;
And on the pedestal these words appear:
'My name is Ozymandias, king of kings:
Look on my works, ye Mighty and despair!'
Nothing beside remains. Round the decay
Of that colossal wreck, boundless and bare,
The lone and level sands stretch far away.

Percy Bysshe Shelley

15

Tree climbers of Pompeii

1 Pre-listening

Task 1 Discussion

- Can you see what has been loaded on to the lorry in the picture below?
- How do they grow?
- Why do you think they have been collected?

Compare your ideas in pairs and then tell the rest of the class what you thought. (You will find out if you were right when you listen to the recording.)

2 Listening

You are going to hear someone telling a story spontaneously. It is similar to Unit 8 in that the speaker is the same and this is another occasion on which she saw someone behaving strangely and did not at first understand what was going on.

Task 1 Getting the outline of the story

Listen to the story once through and write down notes which give the general points of the story. Use the questions on the next page to help you.

1 Where the incident took place: . . . .

2 When it took place: . . . .

3 What exactly did she see? (Put appropriate notes in the picture.)

Task 2   Listening for more detail

Listen again and give more details. Use the framework below to help you.

1 What were the men collecting? . . . .

. . . .

2 What part of it was
going to be extracted? . . . .

. . . .

3 What is its use? . . . .

4 What did the questioner expect the use to be? . . . .

. . . .

5 Exactly how were these things collected? . . . .

. . . .

3 Follow-up

Task 1 Echoing

There are two people involved in the telling of this story—the main speaker (A), the person who had the experience and her friend (B), who has not heard the story before and is clearly interested.

B shows her interest by intervening from time to time with a comment or an expansion of what A is saying, for example:

A   ... of course what you go to Pompeii for is the archaeology.
B   *To see the ruins.*

A often shows her approval of B's 'joining in' by repeating (or 'echoing') what B says before she continues with the story, for example

A   ... of course what you go to Pompeii for is the archaeology.
B   To see the ruins.
A   *To see the ruins.* And I was actually seeing the ruins but ...

This often happens in conversation and discussion.

Listen again and write down other examples of 'echoing'.

. . . .

Check your examples with the rest of the class. (You will have the opportunity to check more fully in Task 3.)

Task 2 Expressing surprise and puzzlement

Speaker A was surprised and puzzled when she first saw the men climbing trees and she reports some of the things she said or thought to herself, for example:

'Goodness, what's going on here ...?'

Listen again and complete these phrases containing other expressions of surprise or puzzlement or interest.

1 'Oh . . . . What's going on here?'
2 'and began to wonder what on . . . . was going on'
3 'This was getting . . . .'
4 'so that was the end of my looking at the ruins for about half an hour. I was too . . . . by this . . . . form of agriculture.'

Task 3 Listening with the transcript

Turn to page 88 and listen again, following on the transcript.

Listen once more without the transcript. Are you now able to 'hear' more of the speaker's words?

KEY

UNIT 1

Section 2

Task 2

A male toad looking for a mate would try to sit in the coldest part of the pond (the central area) where its croak would be deepened. Alternatively a clever toad might sit on the bank and try to catch a female en-route to the centre!

Most attractive: B   Least attractive: A

Task 3

| 1 Male toad sits in cold water. | 2 Cold water lowers his body temperature. | 3 Lower temperature deepens his voice. |

4 Female toad is attracted to him.

Section 3

Task 1

smallest, warmer, shriller, less enticing

Task 2

| Libby Purves | Times |
| Fairchild | Duke |

for, to, the, of, to, on, the, of, be, the, to

UNIT 2

Section 2

Task 1

	Person's job	Prejudice about the job
1	Civil Service	'grey' (i.e. boring)
2	head of department in a company	assume jobholder is male
3	nursing officer	assume nurses are normally female; male ones must be failed doctors
4	bank manager	stuffy, bourgeois image
5	sales representative	not very dependable
6	apprentice hairdresser	looked down on as being for 'dim' girls

Task 4

physicists, lawyers, economists, accountants, sales representatives, estate agents, biologists, mechanical engineers, electrical engineers, civil engineers.

Task 6

2 low status	7 interesting company
3 subordinate	8 badly dressed
4 insecure	9 hardworking
5 well paid	10 reliable
6 interesting	11 friendly
	12 cheerful

Task 7

1 lawyer
2 accountant
3 physicist
4 biologist
5 economist
6 civil engineer
7 electrical engineer
8 mechanical engineer
9 sales representative
10 estate agent

Section 3

Task 1

as against, rather than

Task 2

take/give; badly/well; gloomy/cheerful

UNIT 3

Section 2

Task 1

1 herbs (basil, majoram, mint), tomatoes, aubergines, courgettes, dwarf beans, lettuce
2 on the terrace
3 the herbs
4 red peppers
5 They grew from seeds which she threw away when cooking with red peppers
6 about twenty
7 She gave them away to friends and kept about three.
8 no
9 Because she is moving to London where the climate is unsuitable.

Section 3

Task 1
success
managed, fine, did OK, I got super tomato plants and
quite nice-looking aubergines, they come up all right,
most of them 'took', they actually were doing rather well,
and they were 'taking' all over the place

failure
semi-disaster, accident, the only trouble was, I must have
miscalculated, none of the things that should have had
flowers, so nothing happened, that was it, they didn't last
too well either, that was the end of that, the courgettes
died, that wasn't too good, a scene of desolation, gave up
on it altogether, In the midst of all this desolation

UNIT 4

Section 2

Task 1
1   Andean Condor
2   Eagle Owl
3   Great Sulphur Crested Cockatoo
4   Mute Swan
5   Raven
6   Green Amazon Parrot

Task 2

1	Andean Condor	74 (at least)	1964	Moscow Zoo
2	Eagle Owl	68	—	UK zoo
3	Great Sulphur Crested Cockatoo	approx 73	—	—
4	Mute Swan	70	—	—
5	Raven	69	—	—
6	Green Amazon Parrot	104	1975	London Zoo

Section 3

Task 1
1   Andean Condor   probably correct
2   Eagle Owl   probably correct
3   Great Sulphur
    Crested Cockatoo   probably correct
4   Mute Swan   probably correct
5   Raven   absolutely correct
6   Green Amazon Parrot   questionable

Task 2
1   'he was probably much more than 74'
2   '68 or more very likely when it died'
3   'probably about 73 when he died'
4   'there's a fairly reliable record of 70 years'
5   'now he was 69 years'
6   'the date of birth isn't really reliable, so one can't be
    absolutely sure'

Task 3
1   No '. . . or some beer if you prefer it.'
2   Yes
3   No '. . . and Hobson.'
4   Yes
5   No '. . . and Friday.'

UNIT 5

Section 2

Task 2
Type of computer owner
1   earnest
2   games players
3   practical   √

Task 3
1   To learn Italian irregular verbs.
2   She couldn't get the program right.
3   She never got the program right but the constant
    typing-in of the irregular verbs meant that she learnt
    them anyway.

Task 4

1	Date file:	stores names, addresses, phone numbers, references to books & articles
2	Home calculator:	helps to work out personal finances — taxes, bills, etc.
3	The writer:	allows you to edit and correct text on a screen before printing it out

UNIT 6

Section 1   Task 1
sight, hearing, touch, smell, taste

Task 3
2   Ooh, yes please.

Section 2

Tasks 1 & 2

1	Autocuer	spectacles fitted with microphone and connected to microcomputer worn on speaker's body. Microphone picks up sound within 12 ft of user, sent to computer for analysis and translated into symbols representing different sounds. Symbols appear in liquid crystal display on one of the lenses.
2	Mini Fonator	worn on the wrist. Has built in microphone and microprocessor. User 'feels' the differences in pitch of voice on his arm.

3   GE Echo 2000   messages tapped out at one end using push-button phone. Appear on a screen at the other end.

4   Telesign   Transmits video images through phone system to a screen at the other end.

Section 3

Task 1

at, and, can, the, to, with

UNIT 7

Section 2

Task 1

are, and, is, will, are, or, will, a, the, in, will, and, is, it, to

Task 3

Situation	Rubber is very important in Malaysia's economy, e.g. 1981 20% GNP, 30% export earnings	
Problems	**2** workers are leaving the land for cities	**1** trees have a useful life of about 30 years
Cause	boredom v. labour intensive	
Possible solutions	raise livestock — chickens, turkeys & especially sheep	insurance schemes for smallholders to assist them when new trees maturing

Task 5

1   20%   2   every other   3   400
4   30   5   about 30 million

Task 6

Type of animal	successful?	reasons
1 chickens	no	profits disappointing
2 turkeys	no	not established part of Malaysian diet
3 sheep	yes	eat weeds/source of meat, milk, wool, skin

Section 3

Task 1

Examples of interruption:
1   **Frobisher** . . . on paper the citizens are richer than those of the UK but . . .
    Benson But of course that wealth . . .
2   **Frobisher** . . . Now I remember my planting days . . .
    Benson Yes, yes, yes, you're quite right there Andrew,
3   **Frobisher** I remember in my day just after . . .
    Benson Yes, most people have this image of vast estates, . . .

Examples of nasty comments:
1   **Benson** . . . Poverty line . . .
    Frobisher . . . Whatever that means . . .

2   **Benson** . . . when it comes to replacing old trees, you'll know about this, Andrew . . .
    (implying that Frobisher himself is like an old tree)
3   **Frobisher** Overhead projector. There wasn't anything wrong with the blackboard in my time, you know . . .
    Benson Ha, ha, no, but this is clearer and neater and up-to-date.
    (implying that Frobisher is not)
4   **Frobisher** Pushy bastard.
Other:
Students might notice loud volume in places in addition to interruption in an attempt to 'drown' the rival's voice, and 'tone of voice'. Dr Benson also sneers a lot.

UNIT 8

Section 2

Task 1

1   country: Italy
    city: Rome
    specific place: Capitol Hill
    other details: picturesque park with superb views over Rome
2   day: Sunday
    time: morning
3   how many people?   two
    their relationship: man & wife (?)
    what exactly
    were they doing?   hanging over a wall, their feet hardly touching the ground. Man pulling at vegetation growing on other side of wall with a stick. Putting the creepers in a polythene bag

Task 2

habits & habitat: grows on old walls, especially ruins
smell: goaty
taste: pungent
use in cookery: in sauces
how is it prepared
for use in cookery: pickled in salt & vinegar

UNIT 9

Section 2

Task 2

1   South-West Asia, approximately 8,000 years ago
2   Ancient Romans
3   60BC–300AD
4   Caseus
5   Increased knowledge of micro organisms and their effect on taste meant process could be industrialized. Cheese was made on a large scale in factories.

UNIT 10

Section 2

Task 1
There are three speakers — two men and a woman.

Task 3
Llama's cheese:	rough, hard	Peru
Goat's cheese:	hard, crumbly, sharp	Greece
Sheep's cheese:	contained live worms	Sardinia

Section 3

Task 1
1 *You know* I've tried llama's cheese.
2 *D'you know* what I really like is that Greek goat's cheese.
3 *Actually* I think the most peculiar cheese I ever had was in Sardinia.

UNIT 11

Section 1

Task 1
bad for eyes, posture, digestion

Section 2

Task 2
abnormalities in pregnancy (which necessitated termination), increased stress, disturbances to vision, constipation, backache, fatigue, short sightedness, itching of the face/dermatitis

Task 3
Physical	*Mental*
abnormality in pregnancy	stress
disturbances to vision	fatigue
constipation	
backache	
short sightedness	
dermatitis	
thrombosis	

Task 4
Amateurs: disturbances to vision, constipation, backache, fatigue, short sightedness, skin complaints
Common to both: disturbances to vision
Professionals: abnormalities in pregnancy, stress
The speaker thinks that amateur users are in greater danger because they use computers in places without safeguards against the hazards.

Task 6
1 Alternative source of light
2 Rest eyes frequently — look at something in distance to give them change
3 Make sure screen is properly tuned

4 Adopt comfortable working position so not screwed up/bent over
5 Get up and walk about — go outside for fresh air

Section 3

Task 1
1	margin		7	monitor
2	heading		8	screen
3	paragraph		9	keyboard
4	line		10	cable
5	word		11	printer
6	letter			

UNIT 12

Section 1

Task 3
— Language hieroglyphics
— Inspiration for good stories — films, novels
— As land of mystery and magic — source of supernatural events and curses
— Mysticism and paranormal — e.g. interest in pyramids

Section 2

Task 1
Topics: magic mumification medicine
People: archaeologists anthropologists

Task 4
In the past	*In the present day*
scientists and museums bought mummies clandestinely — black market in them	moral scruples — hesitation about carrying out a lot of autopsies on mummies indiscriminately

Task 5
	Ethical	*Practical*
Reasons why scientists are careful	*Dislike of disturbing the dead*	*Any analysis involves some degree of destruction*
Ways in which they show their care	*Mummies restored to state of decent burial after tests*	*Use mummies already in poor condition Take tiny samples Use non-destructive means of study, e.g. X-ray*

UNIT 13

Section 2

Task 1
anthropologists doctors dentists radiologists
microbiologists botanists

Task 2

1	Detroit	early 1970s	
2	Manchester	1975	
3	Paris	1976	Rameses II — 3rd Pharoah of 19th dynasty

Task 3
1	Medical condition —	diseases, av. age of death
2	Physical appearance —	height, weight, build, facial features
3	Process of mummification —	what they did, substances they used

Section 3

Task 1
Rameses II reigned 1290–1224BC (67 years)
He was the third pharoah of the nineteenth Dynasty.

UNIT 14

Section 2

Task 1
1 *Medical condition* Life expectancy 30–35 years though nobility lived longer (Rameses II was over 90). No malignant tumours. No dental decay but teeth eroded because of grit in bread. (Rameses had abscess on jaw.) Intestinal parasites common. Widespread anaemia. Lesions on lungs because of sandy environment.

2 *Appearance* Light and slight — 1.60m tall, 10–15 kg lighter than people of same height today.

3 *Mummification* Different methods which were not always successful. Basic procedure — internal organs removed & preserved separately. (Rameses's nose broken when brain removed, his heart left in situ.) Body immersed in natron (sodium carbonate) 40–70 days, washed, made up (Rameses' hair was dyed) and wrapped in linen bandages. Put in coffin and soaked in more oils, resins and perfumes to help preserve it further.

Task 2
Rameses II
1 1290–1224BC
2 over 90
3 had abscess on jaw

4 heart left in place, face made up. Nose re-structured because damaged when brain removed (stuffed with bones of small animals and peppercorns). Hair dyed
5 much later tomb than his real date
6 been moved and re-buried by priests to hide him from tomb robbers
7 put on display in the Cairo Museum
8 started to deteriorate because of changed atmospheric conditions
9 temporarily moved to Paris for investigation and restoration
10 in controlled environment (back in Cairo Museum)

Section 3

Task 2
Although some very old individuals were encountered . . .
some of them have been found to be 50 or 60 years old
the more medical problems were encountered
some modern disorders have so far not been found
The stones on which their flour was ground
people . . . could have been confined to a liquid diet
traces of what appeared to be tobacco were found
it wasn't always done in the same way
Many bodies were almost entirely destroyed
most of the internal organs . . . were removed and preserved
The brain was got out through the nose
the heart was always removed too.
it was found in place
The body was then immersed
It was then washed, made up and wrapped in . . . and placed in its coffin.
Then it was soaked in oils.
You said the body was made up.
Do you mean its face was painted?
Rameses was not only made up.
. . . which was damaged.
it had been stuffed with small animal bones
His hair had been dyed too.
he was found in a much later tomb
His body was transported
it was put on display
Rameses was specially treated and then rewrapped
given a new sarcophagus and . . . transported back to
he is now kept
not only was science served
proper respect was paid
(The passives are also shown in italics on the transcript on page 87.)

UNIT 15

Section 2

Task 1
1 Pompeii, Italy
2 While she was walking round some ruins into a group of pine trees

3a a man halfway up a tree
  b lorry loaded with pine cones
  c polythene bucket
  d pine cones
  e Roman ruin

Task 2
1 pine cones
2 nut
3 ground up and used in pesto sauce, cakes, sweets
4 fuel
5 cones pulled from trees using a stick with hook at one end

Section 3

Task 1
'shinned up the tree'
'it's quite a delicacy'
'much more interesting'

Task 2
1 'goodness'
2 'earth'
3 'ridiculous'
4 'fascinated', 'strange'

TEXT OF THE RECORDINGS

UNIT 1

Cold toads   (2'04")

. . . Let me offer you, at about fourth hand, quite the most enjoyable item of news to come my way during the past week.

I heard it from my colleague Libby Purves, who read it in *The Times* newspaper, which got it ultimately from Dr L Fairchild of Duke University in North Carolina and it concerns toads.

The female toad, unaware of spiritual values, likes her mate big. But because she normally pairs in the dark, she has only one way of judging. The bigger the toad, the deeper his croak. However, there's a complicating factor, because a cold toad gives a deeper croak. Male toads therefore cunningly make for the coldest corner of the pond to deepen their croaks, and a female, who thinks she is mating with a large, warm toad may in fact have been deceived by a small, cold one.

However, things do not stop there. Since all the male toads are trying to chill off as much as possible, the large ones tend to win in the end and take over the cold spot. Indeed, says Dr Fairchild, many of the smallest toads are forced right out of the pond and are obliged to sit on the bank where (since it is warmer out of the water than in, even in North Carolina) the small toads' croaking becomes even shriller and less enticing.
But there is still some consolation for the warm weaklings. For in order to get into the pond the females do, of course, have to run the gauntlet on the bank where, says Dr Fairchild, the small males make the most of their opportunities. It shouldn't be long before the large toads learn to lurk on the bank and shut up.

My problem now is how to . . .

UNIT 2

Job stereotypes

Part 1   (3'23")

1   When I was at university, I was — I was horrified by what had happened to a lot of my friends by the time they reached the end of the course. Having spent their university careers being all the things one is at university — clever, artistic, very noisy — at the end of their time they all seemed to take entry exams for the . . . the Civil Service, and there were some of them who went . . . huh . . . went as low as to go into the Tax Office huh. How grey, how grey, I thought. But now huh, well, look at me!

2   The circular letters I get drive me absolutely mad, from American Express, etc. They're sent to my work address and they're all addressed to *Mr* S Andrews! Obviously they found the name on some published list and assumed that anybody who wasn't a secretary must of course be a man. It's stupid really, because the Company does put Mr or Ms in front of the names on its departmental lists, but perhaps because they naturally assume it's a man, they're just blind to the women's names amongst the heads of departments.

3   I work in London at er . . . a large hospital as a nursing officer. It's erm . . . it's what a lot of people call a male nurse, which I think is the most ridiculous term I've ever come across. It . . . sort of implies that a nurse ought to be female and that by being male I'm different, but er . . . the idea still carries on. The other thing is that people always say 'I suppose you really wanted to be a doctor', just because I'm a man. They can't imagine that I really wanted to be a nurse and that er . . . erm . . . it wasn't just that I failed to be a doctor. And . . . what they don't realize is the work's completely different, you know as a . . . a male nurse you've much more contact with the er . . . patients and, you know, a long term responsibility for their . . . their welfare. huh There's no way I'd want to be a doctor. Well, except for the money of course.

4   Whenever I say I'm a bank manager, half the time people tend to laugh. I've never understood why. I suppose bank managers do have a rather stuffy bourgeois image, but I can't see why it's funny.

5   I'm a sales representative, what used to be called a travelling salesman, and for some reason there's lots of dirty jokes about travelling salesmen. Can't think why. Well, I suppose it's because they tend to travel a lot, you know, a night here, a night there. Well, people get the idea they're not particularly dependable, sort of fly by nights I suppose, you know, wife in every port. But it aint true, I promise you.

6   I'm an apprentice hairdresser. I enjoy the work very much. I'm learning a lot, not just about hair, but how to get along with people. I'm gaining confidence 'cos I never had that at school. I left as soon as I could. I hated it. I remember teachers used to look down on jobs like hairdressing. They were ever so stuck up. They thought that only girls who were a bit dim went in for hairdressing, but I'm not dim at all. If I work hard in the salon and get all my certificates, if I save

hard, in a few years I could start my own business, and I'd be earning five times as much as those old bags at school!

Part 2

Section 1   (1'41")

Interviewer Well, we heard some people just now who seem to feel that other people have a wrong idea about the work they do. Do you think this sort of thing is very widespread?

Sociologist Oh absolutely. Most jobs or professions seem to have an image or a stereotype attached to them, often much to the irritation of the job-holders. But there is a serious point to all this, too, that maybe young people actually choose their careers under the influence of these false images. And certainly, there is evidence that they may even avoid certain careers because they have a negative image. Well, on a large scale, as you can imagine, this could cause problems for whole sectors of the economy.

Interviewer Er, you say there's evidence?

Sociologist Oh most definitely. There was a survey recently into children's attitudes to different professions.

Interviewer How was that done, though? Because, after all, children don't know much about the world of work before they get into it.

Sociologist Well, exactly. What the investigators wanted to get at was their impressions and their prejudices. They used a very simple technique. They gave the children twelve pairs of statements. In each pair one statement was positive, the other was its opposite.

Interviewer For example?

Sociologist Well, for example, 'Such and such a person is likely to be boring or interesting company'.

Interviewer I see. What professions did they ask about?

Sociologist (laugh) Do you want the whole list?

Interviewer Well, why not?

Sociologist OK. Here goes. They looked at: physicists, lawyers, economists, accountants, sales representatives, estate agents, biologists, and three types of engineer — mechanical engineers, electrical and civil. The children were asked to say which of the statements was 'most true' about each profession.

Section 2   (1'04")

Interviewer And the results?

Sociologist Well, they were rather striking concerning one profession in particular, the poor old engineer. Of all the jobs mentioned, he came out really much worse than you might expect. The vast majority of children (90% in the case of the mechanical engineer), thought that engineering was a 'dirty job'. They also thought the job was of 'low status' and 'subordinate'; that is, the engineer is more likely to take orders than to give them. Oh, and insecure too. The only other person they thought more likely to actually lose his job was the sales representative. But, I must say there were good points too. Engineering was seen to be 'interesting, well paid' work.

Interviewer Hmm, not such a rosy picture, really.

Sociologist No . . . but it got better when the children were asked about how they imagined the engineer as a person. The majority of the children chose positive comments, except that they thought the engineer was likely to be *badly* rather than *well dressed*. (laugh)

Section 3   (1'50")

Interviewer Well, what about the other professions, then? Erm . . . what came out favourite, for example?

Sociologist Oh the lawyer without a doubt. He collected by far the greatest number of positive opinions. The sales representative and then the estate agent were right at the bottom.

Interviewer Oh, so the engineers weren't right down there?

Sociologist Oh no! The children's ratings put them just above the poor old sales representative all bunched together. Probably the children don't have that much of an idea of their real work. I think they . . . (laughs) . . . they went by the titles, really, since civil engineer came out top, perhaps the suggestion of the name?

Interviewer Oh, I see. You mean that he was a . . . a more civilized sort of chap than the others?

Sociologist (laughs) Yes, right. Reasonable sounding, isn't it?

Interviewer Yes. Quite sensible, I suppose. And I imagine the mechanical engineer came out bottom?

Sociologist Absolutely right. In fact 90% of the children associated him with *dirty work*, as against 76% for the electrical engineer and 68% for the civil engineer.

Interviewer And the other professions?

Sociologist Well, after the lawyer came the accountant; then the scientists, the physicist first. The economist came just above the engineers. Funnily enough, he was the only one that the majority of children felt would be *gloomy* rather than *cheerful*.

Interviewer A real sign of the times, that.

Sociologist Yes. But I still think the most serious implication of the results of the survey was the children's apparent ignorance of the importance of the engineer's role in society.

Interviewer Hmm.

Sociologist After all, in most other European countries to be an engineer is to be somebody. And I imagine that this means that many bright children, who might really enjoy the profession and do well in it, probably never consider it, which is a great pity for the country as a whole. We do need good engineers after all.

Part 3   (0'27")

. . . they also thought that the job was of 'low status' and 'subordinate' that is the engineer is more likely to take orders than to give them . . .

. . . the majority of the children chose positive comments except that they thought the engineer was likely to be 'badly' rather than 'well dressed'.

. . . Funnily enough, he was the only one that the majority of children felt would be 'gloomy' rather than 'cheerful'.

UNIT 3

Hot stuff (5'13")

Woman Well, it's like my bloody red peppers. Did you . . .?

Man What bloody red peppers?

Woman Well, I think you had some last year.

Man That little pot?

Woman I gave you that plant, didn't I?

Man Yeh.

Woman Yes.

Man Yes.

Woman I don't know what happened to it.

Man It died.

Woman Yes. Well . . . Well, anyway, that was one of my, my enormous harvests I got last year.

Man What from your your terr . . .?

Woman From my terrace, yes. It was, it was a case of a totally unexpected sort of semi disaster accident.

Man What . . . Tell me . . . How did that happen?

Woman Well, it's a nice, it's a nice terrace. It gets the sun.

Man Uh mm.

Woman So I thought now's my chance. At last I can indulge all my fantasies of doing a nice bit of urban gardening, you know . . .

Man Right.

Woman . . . how it is. If you're, if you're a town person, you always want to grow your own food. I, I'm not very interested in flowers myself. I, I like growing things I can eat or things I can use but

Man OK.

Woman So, anyway . . .

Man So you decided to grow some red peppers.

Woman Well, I didn't, actually, I decided to grow nice things like, um, herbs, like basil and, er . . .

Man Yeh.

Woman . . . marjoram and, er, um, mint, you know, the usual things. And I also got, rather ambitious and thought, well, tomatoes, that's not ambitious . . .

Man Tomatoes are the . . .

Woman Tomatoes you can grow anywhere. I've managed before, even in London, and not just . . . So, I thought, Italy's ideal. So I also went, um, and got some seeds for things like aubergines and, um . . .

Man That's quite adventurous.

Woman No, no, 'cos you can grow aubergines in . . . As long as you've got a large pot and enough earth . . . And I also bought tons of fertilizer, you know, guano and . . .

Man Guano?!

Woman Yes, that's what it says on the packet — guano — ideal for tomatoes and other vegetables. And I got courgettes and, er oh, even some beans.

Man What kind of beans?

Woman Well, not, not the big ones, not, not the broad beans . . .

Man Runner beans.

Woman . . . but not runner beans. They're . . . It's a sort of er dwarf bean that you can, er . . .

Man Dwarf bean!

Woman Yes, it grows about three feet high and you can . . .

Man Not very dwarf!

Woman Well, for a bean it's a dwarf.

Man OK.

Woman You can grow it up a piece of string.

Man Uh mm.

Woman So I thought, well, do that as well. So I got all these things, and a bit of lettuce as well.

Man Lettuce?!

Woman Yes, well, that's all right. It doesn't need much earth. So I, I sowed all these things and I waited . . .

Man Mm.

Woman And, you know, there we were, and they came up.

Man Great.

Woman Yes, they came up and, well, the mint and the, erm and the herbs in general, the marjoram and the, um, and the basil, were fine and did OK and I got, ooh, super tomato plants, and quite nice-looking aubergines and . . .

Man God, you're really lucky. I've never grown anything from from seed at all.

Woman No, no, no. They come up all right but the only trouble was that I must have miscalculated with the fertilizer.

Man What, the guano?

Woman The guano, yes. Because none of the things that should have had flowers, like the, um . . .

Man Um.

Woman . . . aubergines and the the courgettes and the the tomatoes seemed to feel the need to have flowers. They were, they were probably too, too . . .

Man They didn't worry about it.

Woman They didn't worry about it, so, of course, if you don't have flowers, you don't get fruit.

Man So, so nothing happened?

Woman Nothing happened. So I just got these wonderful, you know, balcony decoration of green leaves.

Man Edible weeds.

Woman Edible weeds. That was it, yes. Well, they didn't all last too well either 'cos the beans grew up the string for a bit, then they gave up and died and grew down again and that was the end of that.

Woman Then I, um I, I went away for the weekend and forgot to water things and the the courgettes died and so . . .

Man Oh dear.

Woman . . . did the aubergines. So that wasn't too good. Yes, so it was rather a scene of desolation.

Man What . . .? So they gave up on it altogether?

Woman Well, they all gave . . . Well, I, I gave up. I thought, well, you know you know just let them stay

there. Anyway, while I was doing all this, um, quite without thinking about it, I was cooking and I I like to use chilli, those red peppers . . .

Man Yeh.

Woman . . . quite a bit and, of course, if you put the whole, the whole red pepper in . . . the food is . . .

Man It goes hot and horrible.

Woman It's quite revolting, isn't it?

Man Mm.

Woman And you can't eat it. So I I er just use the outside part. So, of course, I had the seeds and, since I was cooking near an open window, and not being particularly tidy, I was just throwing the seeds out of the window.

Man Out of the window?

Woman And you can imagine where they landed.

Man On the terrace, on the balcony.

Woman On the terrace, on the earth, yes.

Man Oh.

Woman And most of them took, it seems. I, I, I couldn't work out . . .

Man Sprouted and everything?

Woman Yes, they did, yes. I I couldn't work out what was happening for about two weeks because in the midst of all this, this desolation of the other things, these these mystery plants were coming up.

Man You mean they were growing?

Woman Yeh, they were growing and in the end I I id. . . identified what they were and they actually were doing rather well and they had flowers, and not only did they had flowers, did they have flowers, but they started having peppers.

Man And this is the red pepper from that . . .?

Woman Yes, and in fact I got so many . . . I got about twenty in the end and they were taking over the place so I, I started giving them away to friends and I kept about three, I suppose, and, er, well, that's the source of my present supply of dried peppers. I've got about five years' worth, I think.

Man But not too many courgettes . . .

Woman Not too many courgettes . . .

Man . . . tomatoes, bananas or other things . . .

Woman . . . tomatoes or anything else, or anything else I paid a lot of money for. I just had these, these free, er, red peppers.

Man There's a lesson there somewhere. The next time you want red peppers, you could sow courgettes and . . .

Woman Well, there is.

Man . . . carrots and then you'll probably get red peppers.

Woman Probably get red peppers, yeh. The trouble is I think, you know, moving back to London next year there's not gonna be much chance because I don't think even the the strongest red pepper is going to survive in that climate.

Man Semi-tropical climate, no, mm.

Woman Anyway, there we are.

Man Well, if you've got a spare red pepper plant, I might . . .

UNIT 4

Old birds

Part 1   Mini dictation   (0'58")

Number one: Andean Condor
Number two: Eagle Owl
Number three: Great Sulphur Crested Cockatoo
Number four: Mute Swan
Number five: Raven
Number six: Green Amazon Parrot

Part 2   (1'50")

Radio presenter Well, let's turn to our next question. Keith Bates writes 'Dear Wildlife Experts, I know that parrots can live to an incredible age. What about other birds?' So, er . . . it's over to you, Alan, for this one, I think.

Expert Yes, well, it's an interesting question, but erm . . . our problem with all questions like this is, how reliable are the records? I . . . I'll have to talk mostly about birds in captivity, but even then we can't always be sure. Erm . . . I'll start with the oldest bird, who . . . whose age has been reliably recorded, and that's an Andean Condor. And one died in Moscow Zoo about er . . . 1964. Now he was at least 74 because he'd been in captivity for 72 years, but then, who knows his age when he was caught? He was adult when he was caught so he was probably much more than 74. And i . . . in Britain there was another zoo bird, an Eagle Owl, 68 or more very likely, when it died. And er . . . there was a Great Sulphur Crested Cockatoo. Now that age wasn't completely verified, but he was probably about 73 when he died. Er . . . a . . . a Mute Swan, now there's a fairly reliable record of 70 years, along with a . . . with a Raven. Now he was 69 years. And . . . and the famous case, Jimmy the Green Amazon Parrot at London Zoo. The claim is that he was born, or rather he was hatched, in captivity in 1871. So, since he died in 1975, well that would be 104, but the date of birth isn't really reliable, so one can't be absolutely sure. You see, the the problem is that zoos don't always have clear records . . .

Part 3   (1'31")

a 1   We've got coffee and tea and coca cola . . .
  2   Well the principal products are rubber and oil . . .
  3   There are useful articles on this subject by Brown, Andrews, Jones, Smith . . .
  4   I suggest you read Brown and Andrews . . .
  5   The clinic is open Monday and Tuesday and Thursday . . .

b 1   We've got coffee and tea and coca cola or some beer if you prefer it.
  2   Well the principal products are rubber and oil.
  3   There are useful articles on this subject by Brown, Andrews, Jones, Smith and Hobson.

4 I suggest you read Brown and Andrews.
5 The clinic is open Monday and Tuesday and
   Thursday and Friday.

UNIT 5

Home computers

Part 1

Section 1 (2′25″)
Annie (laugh) That's wonderful. That's really good.
Man You've got one, haven't you, Annie?
Annie Yes, I have.
Man Well, how do you find it?
Annie Er, well . . . I'm not . . .
Man Round the corner, through the shops . . .
Annie (laugh) I'm not sure it's really me somehow.
(Oh . . .) Well . . .
Man Just your style.
Annie Well, home-computer owners fit into three main
categories. You see, (oh yes.) there are the earnest
ones, the games players, and the practical ones.
Man Oh yes, what do you mean?
Annie Well, earnest ones, they sort of work away at
learning how to program the thing for themselves. Er
. . . then games players, they get hooked on playing
those silly games you can buy and don't do much else. I
call them silly games because I'm not co-ordinated
enough to be good at them myself. Then, thirdly the
practical ones, and that's me. (Oh yes?) I don't use the
computer very often, but I have worked out some ways
in which it can be helpful in everyday life. (Sounds
marvellous). Well, I started off as an earnest computer
owner, but I gave up being like that because of lack of
success with programing.
Man Like with the games.
Annie Exactly. Well you know how easily I give up. But
this time it was going to be different. I tried and tried
but I had so many disasters. I blamed it on the
instruction book. It was awful, not not clear at all.
Man Disasters, eh?
Annie Well yes. You know that I had that Italian exam to
take?
Man Mm. I remember.
Annie Well, I'd read a lot about how computers were
useful in language teaching for giving boring but
necessary grammar practice. Well, I had to learn a lot
of Italian irregular verbs. (Sounds lovely.) So, I decided
to try and write a program to help me. Well, actually
what I did was, I I tried to adapt a program for French
verbs found in a computer magazine.
Woman Gosh, aren't you clever!
Man And . . . the computer didn't like Italian as much as
French! (laugh) It didn't work.
Annie No. Well, in a way it did, but not as I expected. I
just couldn't get the program right. The verbs kept
appearing on the screen, but jumping all over the place.
It was quite alarming really.

Man It sounds like space invaders to me. (laugh) What
happened?
Annie Well, I tried again and again to get the program
right. I kept altering it and testing it, which meant
typing in all the list of verbs I wanted to learn each time
I tested. (Cor.) Well, the result was, the program
never came quite right, I gave up in disgust. But, after
all those repetitions I found I'd learned the verbs
perfectly! It was nothing to do with the bloody program!
It was just all those hours spent trying to sort it out!
(laugh.)

Section 2 (2′08″)
Man So now you . . . you've stopped being earnest and
become practical, have you? Er, what does that mean
exactly, by the way?
Annie Well, it means I've stopped trying to invent my
own programs and I've started buying other people's.
Well, there are thousands of programs on cassette in
the shops. I found three in particular that have made my
life easier.
Man Oh yeah, what are those?
Annie Well, so far I've collected a tape that lets me store
things like names and addresses and phone numbers, or
references to books and articles. Er . . . I think that's
called Datafile. Then there's one that helps me work
out personal finances. (Ah, that sounds all right) That's
wonderful — taxes, bills, you know . . . The . . . it's
called The Home Calculator. But, the best buy so far is
a word processing program. It's called The Writer.
That lets you type a letter, or anything you like, just as
you would normally only it appears on the TV screen
first. (Gosh.) Then you can look at it and make
adjustments on the screen or, or correct mistakes of
course . . .
Man Oh, I could do with one of those.
Annie But, you can delete whole chunks. You can move
the position of whole sections, and change the layout.
(Sounds wonderful). Have a wider or a narrower
margin, you see. It's only when you're quite happy with
it that you need to put it on to paper, just by pressing
one key. Then the whole perfect finished product is
printed out.
Woman Oh, how wonderful!
Annie It is, it's fantastic! Not just because you can save
paper and time but because it's so fascinating that you
spend hours on things that would normally, you get
bored with very quickly. And the appearance is
fabulous, contrary what . . . to what some people would
think. (Oh . . . yes, I thought so, yeah . . .) And
goodbye to all those disgusting drafts, you know. Well,
I know there are dire warnings about spending too
much time crouched over a computer keyboard, (Oh
yeah?) they, well yes, they say it's bad for your eyes,
and bad for posture.
Man Yea, well it's the same with a typewriter, isn't it?
Annie Well, yes, bad for digestion you know.
(Digestion?) (laugh) You find that it saves so much in
time and frustration, using other people's programs,

not your own, of course, that your blood pressure must at least benefit.

Man So, are you going to have another go at doing your own programs now?

Annie Oh no, not for a long time. I'm quite happy being a parasite.

Woman (laugh) You lazy thing!

Part 2

Section 1 (3′55″)

Shelagh . . . Well I think home computer owners fit into three main categories really er the ones I call the earnest ones — the sort of people who work away at learning to write their own programs — who who really want to know how the computer works um the ones who end up mainly playing silly games on the computer. I say 'silly games' cos I'm I'm not co-ordinated enough ever to um to do well at any any of those sorts of things. I'm just useless at the games. . . . and the ones I call the practical ones. That's me um who probably don't use their computers very often, um but they've worked out a few ways in which er the computer, the computer can help them in in their everyday lives or, or with their work, perhaps.

um I've had my computer about two years and I haven't really used it that much um. I started off as an earnest owner but I, I very quickly gave up that attitude because I, I just wasn't doing very well um with the programing. I er of course I blamed it on the instruction book um but I had so many er hilarious disasters um with my attempts to program that that that I gave it up for a while um wha-

Liz It's always the program that got away, isn't it?

Shelagh Well, absolutely. um The trouble is unless you have a deep understanding of what's going on — well in my case the only way to see if a program you think you've written is working is to try it out which means doing it typing it again and again into the machine and then running it to see if it will work. So you can spend hours doing this. um One example is um I er tried to write myself a program that would help me learn some er Italian verbs 'cos I'm interested in in learning languages and I actually had an Italian exam that I had to take and I knew I I would have to know um the past tense of some particular verbs which were irregular ones, um so I thought well, it would be more amusing if I could write myself um a program um so that um I could have the, let's say the infinitive of the verb would come on the screen and then I would type in what I thought the past tense was and the computer would tell me if I was right or wrong, so it would be a sort of game but er an educational game. I um I tried, I I found a similar program in a a computer magazine and I tried to copy it or or adapt it but I just couldn't get it right and the idea was that the infinitive of the verb would come on the screen and then I'd type in the answer but there was something terribly wrong with my pro- I don't know because it was getting quite frightening because these verbs were appearing on the screen anywhere. I didn't know where they were coming next. They were jumping all over the screen and then I would put in my answer and

the answer would jump all over the place and it it really was um it was getting quite alarming. And of course I was doing it again and again trying to get it right and of course the result was that I I repeated these verbs I I was trying to put into the computer so often so often that by the time I'd done it for several hours, I'd learnt the verbs anyway. I didn't need the program. So I thought it would be a good idea to write an article for a language teaching journal um pointing out how much you can learn from your computer just by being useless at programing for it because um I certainly learnt my verbs that way.

Section 2 (4′12″)

So um after a few experiences like that, I gave up being earnest and and trying to write my own programs and decided to become practical and I I simply bought um cassettes of other people's ready-made programs for purposes that I thought would be useful to me. Of course, you're rather limited to to what actually is available on the market and you may not find exactly what you want but um I've got three commercially available er programs which have actually made my life easier er in quite a number of ways. er So far I've got a tape that lets me store information — things like names and addresses or references to books and articles in a in an organized way er rather as if you were doing it on file cards. I-it's called er Data File I think. um I've got another one which helps me with er my personal finances — calculating taxes, adding up bills, keeping records of um of er bills, electricity bills, things like that. That's called The er Calculator. But my, my best buy so far has been er a word processing program er I think that's called Writer, just Writer. That lets me type in a text just as I would on a, on a normal typewriter only of course it comes up initially on the TV screen not on paper, er and then I can play about with it. I can change it, I can move words around, I can correct mistakes, I can even move or delete whole paragraphs or, if I want to, I can change the margin or, or the numbers, or the numbers of letters in a line. And it's only when I'm quite happy with my text that er I need to print it out actually on to paper.

And that's fantastic for me because not only have I saved about a ton of paper because normally I'm, I'm a really very untidy writer, I I do things again and again and I cross things out etc., but I find the um

but I find the process absolutely fascinating I can sit for hours in front of the screen just working on on something that I'd get bored with normally. I- I- It's quite an hy a hy hypnotic effect um because you have all that power over what happens on the screen and once you've changed something there's no messy correction or crossing out. It it looks all beautiful and er very satisfactory.

And I'm sure that um I'm motivated to to to do much more work on any article or or letter that I'm writing than um I would just with a pen and paper and I'm sure the result um in terms of content and — as well as as appearance is is always um much superior to what I would um produce normally. It's a fabulous feeling. You just press the right key when you're ready and the whole thing is printed out

all neat and beautiful. It was quite expensive to buy the printer which produces the um the actual printed paper um version of the text but um at least it was goodbye to all those disgusting looking typescripts and drafts that I used to produce. I know there are um dangers and there are many dire warning issued about spending too much time crouched over a computer, that they say it's bad for your eyes, bad for your posture, bad for your digestion, you name it um but I've, I've find I've saved so much in frustration, I'm sure my blood pressure must be much lower while I'm working on something compared with the old methods er typewriter, correcting fluid, etc. I expect I'll get back to um trying to do my own pro- programing sometime, um but at the moment I'm just happy being a parasite using other people's programs um in a way that um is actually helping me and saving me time.

UNIT 6

Glasses that hear   (5'13")

Presenter So, now, 'Can we help you?' turns to its regular new technology spot. Well, this week we're looking at ways in which deaf and hard-of-hearing people can be helped to make the most of the skills they already have in order to communicate more easily with other people. I'm asking our resident expert, Dr Ronald Harper, to fill us in on what's new and on what lies ahead. So, Ron, can we start with the problem of understanding speech? Many deaf and hard-of-hearing people are already skilled in lip-reading. Has technology any role at all to play there?

Expert Well, yes, indeed, and er . . . a very important and interesting one, in that the devices I've been looking at are designed to boost and add a new dimension to skills the deaf person already has, rather than er . . . aiming to replace them.

Presenter Well, how do you mean?

Expert Well, none of the devices I've seen works by itself. They all provide additional information about the speech-signal, the . . . the sort that the deaf person cannot get through his lip-reading skills alone. And er used together with er the information taken in by a good lip-reader, they could bring the user nearer to 100% efficiency.

Presenter And what type of information do you mean?

Expert Well, erm . . . one of the problems about lip-reading, is that so many sounds look the same when you look at the speaker's lips. It's hard to tell many English vowels apart just by looking at the shape of a person's lips, and . . . er consonant sounds like /m/ and /b/ . . . er they're made with the lips in the same position. Er . . . you can often work out what is being said by using the context, but not always, you see, and er there's a splendid new device on the market which helps with this. It's called . . . er it's called the 'Autocuer' and, in fact, it's a pair of spectacles, er but spectacles — and this is the this is the catch — they're spectacles which 'hear'. Er . . . they're fitted with a tiny

microphone, and they're connected to a microcomputer — what else? that is worn on the speaker's body. And the microphone picks up sounds within a range of 12 feet of the user. Now these sounds are sent to the computer for analysis. It then sends up er . . . a series of symbols representing different sounds, which appear in a liquid crystal display on one of the lenses of the glasses where the user can see them. Er . . . once the user has learned which sounds the symbols stand for, he can use them to help sort out one sound from another as he carries on with his normal lip-reading.

Presenter Sounds ingenious.

Expert It is, indeed.

Presenter Well erm . . . are there any other areas in which er lip-reading skill can be assisted?

Expert Well, yes. Er there's the vital area that most hearing people take for granted, what we call 'tone of voice', erm . . . pitch, emphasis, rhythm and so on. These add so much meaning to the bare words we hear, and anything that can help deaf people perceive them better is obviously going to help them. Now, there's a device developed by a German firm, called the Mini-Phonator. Now, this translates acoustic signals into vibrations which vary with the pitch and volume of the speaker's voice, and can be felt on the skin. The Mini-Phonator is . . . is worn on the wrist like a watch, and like the Autocuer has a microphone built in and, yes, a microprocessor that is worn on the user's body.

Presenter Extraordinary. Well, Ron, what about the other side of the communication coin, speaking to other people?

Expert Yes, well, now, face to face many deaf people are extremely good at this already, and in many cases they have the additional possibility of using sign language. However, communicating over long distances has up to now posed a problem. Er, and it's ironical that the telephone, an instrument most deaf people cannot use, was the result of research whose first intention was to help the deaf. Both Alexander Graham Bell and his father were famous teachers of the deaf.

Presenter Were they really?

Expert Mm, yes. But now there some . . . there are some devices which at last make the use of the phone feasible for the deaf and the hard-of-hearing. And one very simple idea is that of the GE Echo 2000, developed by the American General Electric Company. Er . . . Now with this, messages can be tapped out in the written form, using a push-button phone, to appear on a screen at the other end. Now, the great plus for this device is that it's also extremely cheap, it's only about $250 at the moment.

Presenter So, it isn't perhaps as fast as the spoken word, but certainly useful to exchange short messages over long distances.

Expert Oh, absolutely yes, quite. I mean, you wouldn't exactly want to have a . . . good long gossip through the GE Echo, but for making decisions and exchanging important information it certainly would make life

easier. However, if the people at both ends of a telephone line know sign language, they *could* have a good gossip, with the help of another device. The 'Telesign' transmits video images in a simplified form through the phone system to a screen at the other end. So, you can follow your friend as he signs to you over the telephone!

Presenter Mmm. So what we have is a whole set of ways of supporting skills that er deaf people may have already developed in their own right.

Expert That's absolutely right and, and and and . . . that's what I think is so interesting. They add information that the person cannot get through his ears, while leaving him with the responsibility of developing his skills of communication, as a whole.

UNIT 7

A post-industrial society

Part 1   (5′38″)

Chairperson Good evening ladies and gentlemen. It's nice to see so many of you here. Well, I'd like to introduce our two guests this evening: Mr Andrew Frobisher, who has spent many years in Malaysia in the 1950s and 60s and knows the country very well indeed. And, on my right, Dr Harry Benson who's an agricultural economist.

Benson Good evening.

Frobisher Good evening.

Chairperson Well, erm . . . the purpose of this evening is to find out more about that fascinating substance, rubber, and the effects that it has on that fascinating country, Malaysia. Erm erm . . . . I believe erm . . . er Mr Frobisher, erm . . . that Malaysia is at the same time an extremely rich and rather poor country. Erm . . . how is this possible?

Frobisher Yes, well, that's quite true, Monica. Malaysia's population is by now over 12 million, and er per head o . . . on paper the the citizens *are* richer than those of the UK. But . . .

Benson But of course that wealth is not so evenly distributed. In fact in 1981, it was estimated that 37% of the population were below the poverty line . . .

Frobisher Yeah, well . . . whatever that means . . . and anyway shouldn't it be, er, *was* below the poverty line.

Benson Yes, of course. Sorry, Andrew.

Frobisher Yes, well, erm . . . as I was saying, er . . . much of Malaysia's wealth is based on rubber. Now, I remember my planting days . . .

Benson Yes, yes, yes yes you're quite right there Andrew. Rubber represents about 20% of the Gross National Product and 30% of export earnings. (Er yes I . . .) This puts Malaysia in a very good position internationally since rubber is an example of what we might call a 'post-industrial industry'.

Frobisher Well, what do you what do you mean by that? I . . .

Chairperson Er . . . excuse me . . . yes, what does that mean?

Frobisher What is a post-industrial erm . . . society?

Benson Most manufacturing industries are based on fossil fuels, for example, coal and oil. Now, the problem is that these will not last forever. They are finite. Sooner or later they will run out! Now, rubber is a natural product. The energy source involved in its creation is sunlight. Now sunlight, we hope, will outlast coal and oil, and best of all, sunlight is free. So, it is much cheaper to produce natural rubber which as we all know comes from trees, than to use up all those fossil fuels, both as fuels and as raw materials, in making synthetic rubber in factories. Rubber is one of the world's strategic products, so you can see what a good position Malaysia is in, and it would help if she could produce more . . .

Chairperson Er . . . well, what stands in the way then?

Frobisher Ah, well, well it's the way they go about cultivating it. You see, I remember in my day just after . . .

Benson Yes, most people have this image of vast estates, centrally run, but that's just not the case, even if almost a quarter of the population is involved, one way and another, with the production of rubber . . .

Frobisher Yeah well, that's if you count the families . . .

Benson Oh yes, yes, yes almost 3 million people are involved, but the picture is a very fragmented one. Do you realize that there are 2 million hectares of land under cultivation for rubber in Malaysia, but that 70% of this area is divided almongst small-holders — half a million of them — who between them produce 60% of the country's rubber?

Frobisher Well, there's nothing wrong with that i . . . in terms of quality of life, though I remember (yes, quite right . . .) just after the war there was . . .

Benson Yes, quite right. But being a smallholder does present problems. For example, when it comes to replacing old trees — you'll know about this Andrew — and the average useful life of a rubber tree is about 30 years, (yes, yes,) this can cause financial problems for the small farmer. The problem is being tackled, however, by some very enlightened insurance schemes available to the smallholder which can give him help through the difficult years. After all, the new trees take some years to mature and start producing rubber.

Frobisher Yes, indeed they do. I . . . I . . .

Benson Look, I've got an overhead projection here, which I think will be useful to make the various problems and their solutions clearer to us all.

Frobisher Overhead projection. There wasn't anything wrong with the blackboard in my time, you know . . .

Benson No, but this is clearer and neater and up-to-date. So, here you see a summary of the position of rubber in Malaysia's economy and here is the first problem, and the solution that has been found through these insurance schemes.

Chairperson Hm, yes, I see. That's really very clear.

Benson Now for the second and really major problem.

Frobisher And may I ask what that is?

Benson Boredom and fatigue.

Frobisher Boredom and fatigue? What?

Chairperson What do you mean by that?

Benson Well, as with so many societies, the young people are leaving the land for the cities, leaving no-one behind to carry on their parents' business. The root cause seems to be simply, boredom. Rubber is just not that entertaining a product to be involved with. It is labour-intensive in the extreme. Each tree on a plantation has to be tapped, by hand, every other day.

Chairperson Tapped?

Benson Yes.

Frobisher Yes, well, we . . .

Benson Yes. The trunk is cut and the latex that comes out is collected in a cup. This is collected on the next day. 400 trees per day is the average figure per worker, which means 800 trees under the care of each worker, ten hours a day. Now, as I said previously, the main problem is that of the boredom. The work is not only hard, it is also mind-blowingly tedious.

Frobisher So, ha . . . have you got any suggestions to make things more interesting for them?

Benson Well, not so much me, but the Malaysians are doing some very good work in this field. One idea is to make the work on the plantations more varied, and and profitable, by introducing other products which are compatible with continuing to grow rubber trees.

Part 2 (2′22″)

Frobisher So, ha . . . have you got any suggestions to make things more interesting for them?

Benson Well, not so much me, but the Malaysians are doing some very good work in this field. One idea is to make the work on the plantations more varied, and and profitable, by introducing other products which are compatible with continuing to grow rubber trees.

Chairperson Yes for example?

Benson Well, the most promising line seems to be to encourage small-holders to raise livestock which can live amongst the trees.

Frobisher Yes, yes, I, I hear they've started trying raising chickens and and turkeys.

Benson Yes, yes, indeed. I have another OHP at this point.

Frobisher Erm . . . OHP?

Benson Overhead projection. . .

Frobisher Ah.

Benson Anyway, you can see here the different types of animals that have been tried. At first sight, chickens seemed ideal. After all, they did originate as jungle birds. However, hmm hmm excuse me, so far the profits on chickens have proved disappointing. The turkey seemed an excellent choice, since it could live amongst the trees living very well off the seeds of the rubber trees, which lie scattered all over the forest floors and are put to no other use. . .

Frobisher Yes yes . . . but, but the turkey, it's hardly an established part of the Malaysian diet!

Benson Exactly! So far the most successful candidate has been the sheep.

Frobisher Sheep?

Benson Now . . . Sheep. Sheep will eat the weeds, which will save the cultivator money and work, and they are a source of meat which is acceptable both to Hindus and Muslims.

Frobisher Yes, well, that's most important in multi-cultural Malaysia.

Benson Yes, yes, and of course they can also be used for their their milk, their their wool and their skins.

Frobisher Yes, of course . . . Mmm.

Benson And now, as you can see on my OHP . . .

Chairperson Well, erm . . . thank you both very very much to both our guests . . .

Well, what lies ahead for Malaysia? Can her researchers and scientists continue to find ways of increasing the rubber yield? Can the labour-intensive and tedious life of the rubber plantation be made interesting and varied enough to capture the young people's interest and stop the migration to the cities?

Well, I'm sure we've all enjoyed and learned a lot from huh what both our guests have had to say. Huh we look forward to the next meeting in the series 'Other lands, other problems' which will be on Monday next. That's at 8.15 and do please come on time.

Frobisher Hmm hmm. Pushy bastard.

UNIT 8

Bottoms up! (3′16″)

Shelagh I remember the weirdest thing that happened was erm . . . once . . . erm . . . up on the Capitol Hill . . . you know the old . . . ancient . . . citadel of of of Rome er which is now rather a picturesque . . . well it's always been picturesque . . . it's rather a picturesque little park — part of it anyway — with a superb view over Rome, and it's a very nice place to go on a Sunday morning and just sit and read your newspaper, and that's exactly what I was doing one morning, quietly minding my own business reading my newspaper, looking up occasionally at the view, and suddenly erm . . . I saw, hanging over the wall which goes round this little garden I was in, well silhouetted against the sky more or less were two huge bottoms (laugh). This man and a woman, I assume they were man and wife, and they were . . . hanging over the wall, feet scarcely on the ground, doing something . . . I I couldn't work out what on earth they were doing. It looked . . . it looked extremely dangerous. Anyway erm being British I was too discreet to go up directly and ask them so I erm . . . went alongside and just looked over the wall to see what they were doing, and erm . . . the man had a stick in his hand and he was pulling around with the stick at some of the vegetation that was erm growing erm on the wall . . . pulling it up and then pulling some parts off and they were they were putting it into a

polythene supermarket bag, and when they'd got a great big bagful and were obviously quite satisfied erm they went off.

So, I thought. OK. So they're they're pulling creepers off the wall. Fine. Why? Anyway I investigated a bit closer and pulled a piece up myself and and looked at it and erm . . . I recognized it and smelt it and what it was . . . erm . . . you know capers?

Liz Yes, Yes, I do.

Shelagh Erm . . . well, I'm only used to seeing them in small glass jars, rather expensive (That's right) to go in sauces, and of course, what they are is the flower buds of a particular sort of creeper. Erm . . . and I smelt this this bud and it really had that distinctive caper smell . . . you know . . . rather goaty (yes, mmm) and erm pungent. (Yes.) So, that was what they were doing. So I went home and looked up capers in my my herb book. And, er . . . it's fascinating. Apparently they . . . they love growing on old walls, particularly Roman ruins, and I later found out that the Capitol is one of the typical places where you go if you're a Roman and you want to collect yourself some capers to take home and then pickle. Erm . . . you you do it in salt and vinegar I think, to (mm) to get the product that they use to. So they were just hanging over this wall getting their Sunday morning bagful of capers to take home and erm . . . pickle to use in their cooking (laugh).

Liz And so did you have a go?

Shelagh Well I picked a few, but I wasn't quite sure what to do with them. (laugh) Anyway, anyway that's the real thing you, you can just go somewhere and see the most extraordinary sights. It's an entertainment in itself.

UNIT 9

Art or technology? (3'09")

Cheese is one of those foods that we tend to take for granted as always having been with us, and it's odd to think that someone somewhere must have discovered the process that takes place when micro-organisms get into milk and bring about changes in its physical and biochemical structure.

Obviously, we don't know who discovered the process, but it's thought that it came from south-west Asia about 8,000 years ago.

Early cheese was probably rather unpalatable stuff, tasteless and bland in the case of the so-called 'fresh cheeses', which are eaten immediately after the milk has coagulated, and rough-tasting and salty in the case of the 'ripened' cheeses, which are made by adding salt to the soft fresh cheese and allowing other biochemical processes to continue so that a stronger taste and a more solid texture result.

The ancient Romans changed all that. They were great pioneers in the art of cheese-making, and the different varieties of cheese they invented and the techniques for producing them spread with them to the countries they invaded. This dissemination of new techniques took place between about 60 BC and 300 AD. You can still trace their influence in the English word 'cheese', which comes ultimately from the Latin word 'caseus', that's C-A-S-E-U-S.

Well, things went on quietly enough after the Roman period with the cheese producers in the different countries getting on with developing their own specialities. It's amazing the variety of flavours you can get from essentially the same process.

At this stage in history, people weren't aware in a scientific way of the role of different micro-organisms and enzymes in producing different types of cheese. But they knew from experience that if you kept your milk or your 'pre-cheese' mixture at a certain temperature or in a certain environment, things would turn out in a certain way. The Roquefort caves in France are an example of a place that was used for centuries for the ripening of a certain sort of cheese, before people knew exactly why they produced the effect they did.

In the nineteenth century, with the increasing knowledge about micro-organisms, there came the next great step forward in cheese-making. Once it was known exactly which micro-organisms were involved in the different stages of producing a cheese, and how the presence of different micro-organisms affected the taste, it was possible to introduce them deliberately, and to industrialize the process.

Cheese started being made on a large scale in factories, although the small producer working from his farm dairy continued to exist and still exists today. Cheese-making moved very much into the world of technology and industrial processes, although, because the aim is still to produce something that people like to eat, there's still an important role for human judgement. People still go round tasting the young cheese at different stages to see how it's getting on, and may add a bit of this or that to improve the final taste. Whatever the scale of production, there is still room for art alongside the technology.

UNIT 10

How disgusting! (1'41")

Part 1

Woman I suppose there's nothing to prevent cheese from being made from any kind of milk. (hmm) Cat, for example. I read about a machine they invented for milking guinea pigs (Oh come on!), but they couldn't get enough milk to make even one cheese I suppose.

Younger man Now . . . Why on earth would they do that?

Woman What? Milk guinea pigs? I don't know. Some research project or another. Anyway, that's irrelevant. As far as I know they weren't going to go in for guinea pig cheese, they just wanted to know about the composition of their milk.

Older man You know, I've tried llama's cheese.

Younger man Well, I think that explains a lot. What was it like? (laugh)

Older man Well, it it was in Peru. It it was rather rough and hard, it wasn't bad really.

Woman Do you know what I really like is that Greek goat's cheese (Oh yes, I do too). Um . . . what's it called? Fetta, isn't it? That's right. (fetta, fetta, that's right, yeah). And it's sort of hard and crumbly, and very sharp, particularly good in the summer.

Younger man Yeah, but it's so acid. I I like it, but it gives gives me a sore mouth if I eat too much of it.

Woman Oh dear, you poor sensitive thing. I didn't know you had such a sensitive tongue.

Younger man You don't know a lot about me!

Woman Actually, I I think the most peculiar cheese I've ever had was in Sardinia. I think it was, I think it was sheep's cheese, but anyway that that's not the point. What they did to this cheese was that they deliberately put little worms to live inside it.

Younger man Oh don't! Please.

Older man Oh dear, oh dear.

Woman You see, and you're supposed to eat the worms as well (Oh no!). And they're . . . they're very small, and I mean it is 90% cheese, so I suppose it's just possible to do, if you don't think about it too much. But the trouble was, they were very much alive and attracted by the light, and they'd coil themselves up and then PING! (Oh look stop, please!), and then they'd leap up into the lamp at night time. It was very funny.

Older man Oh, it's disgusting actually.

Younger man Well, you didn't need a cabaret afterwards, did you?

Woman Especially when one landed on my friend's bald head! (laugh)

Older man Oh dear! (laugh)

Part 2

Little Miss Muffet
Sat on a tuffet
Eating her curds and whey.
There came a big spider
That sat down beside her
And frightened Miss Muffet away.

UNIT 11

My computer makes me sick!

Part 1 (3′40″)

There's no doubt that the computer has enlarged man's working capacity as well as his intellectual capacity enormously. Er . . . but it brings with it dangers to match the benefits. Now by this, I mean danger to physical and mental well-being of the people who work at computer terminals, not the dangers to personal privacy or national or industrial security.

There's one very alarming set of statistics which come from a survey done in the UK on 800 pregnant women, who happened to use computer terminals for a major part of their working day. In no less than 36% of the subjects there was some severe abnormality during the pregnancy, enough to make a termination necessary. Now these figures compare significantly with a control group of pregnant women of the same age but who did not work with computer terminals. The incidence of severe abnormalities in their case was only 16%. This survey confirms similar investigations carried out in Denmark, Canada, Australia and the USA. Now, no one yet has a clear idea about the exact connection between working with computer terminals and the problems with pregnancy, but the figures at least suggest that there's, well, a cause for alarm.

In more general terms, increased stress and disturbances to vision have been noted in workers exposed for long periods to the video screen, and in many countries trade unions of workers involved with computers have laid down their own guidelines to protect members' health. Erm . . . for instance, rest periods, or a change of activity from time to time are recommended, and the terminal should be placed so that there's a source of natural light, and something else to look at, emm, no blank walls behind the terminal, in other words, so that the operator has a chance to rest his eyes from time to time.

Ironically, it seems that it's not only those who work with computers who are at risk. Er . . . there's perhaps more danger for people who use computers for interest or pleasure in their own homes. Now, it's obviously not possible to impose in the privacy of people's homes the sort of safeguards that can be applied in the working environment. Most people get so fascinated by what they are doing that they stay in front of the screen for hours on end; some are real fanatics!

But they're also using their computers in environments which are not specially designed. Er they may be dusty or hot, and not particularly well-lit on the whole.

An English magazine for computer enthusiasts recently ran its own survey. The readers were invited to send in an account of any health problems they felt were connected with the use of their computers. Er, interestingly, a long list emerged of complaints both serious and less serious, ranging from constipation because of the long hours spent in sedentary ac. . . inactivity, and backache due to crouching over an inconveniently positioned keyboard, erm, right through to a general sense of fatigue owing to having puzzled over a problem for longer than was sensible.

The visual disturbances mentioned above were also very common. Some readers who already suffered from short sight found that the condition had worsened, and a rarer complaint, but still one suffered by a significant number, was an itching of the face, which in some cases became a form of dermatitis. It seems that this is due to the electrostatic field of the video screen attracting dust from

the atmosphere, which irritates exposed skin. And . . . this is an example of a complaint which is rare in the work situation because there is usually some form of air-conditioning, and quite simply not so much dust and fluff in the air as in a normal home.

Part 2   (1′14″)

Precautions for both types of terminal users remain essentially the same. So, first of all, make sure that there's an alternative source of light from that of the screen itself. Secondly, rest your eyes frequently, if possible looking at something in the distance to give them a change from the close focus used on the screen. Thirdly, make sure the screen is properly tuned; a shaky or fuzzy image can cause nausea or headaches. Fourthly, make sure your seat and working area are designed so that you're sitting in a comfortable position, not er . . . screwed up or bent over. And finally, get up regularly and walk about the room. Better still, go out into the fresh air occasionally. Sitting still for hours on end is the best way to encourage a thrombosis in the legs, as well as not being particularly good for the digestion.

These are all common-sense precautions, but how many home-computer owners wrapped up in the intricacies of some programing problem, or fascinated by some game, are going to remember to use their common sense? Does a generation of short-sighted, constipated, hunched, migraine sufferers with skin problems and circulatory troubles await us?

UNIT 12

Mummy dust   (2′49″)

Presenter Today we're going to look at some aspects of life — or perhaps it would be more correct to say 'death' in Ancient Egypt.

Egypt has always fascinated ordinary people as well as scholars engaged in the serious study of the past. To most of us it's a land of mystery and magic. In particular, the custom of preserving the bodies of important people, especially of kings and queens, has quite a hold on the popular imagination. How many thrillers and horror films are based on the idea of finding a mummy in the secret tomb of a lost king, who in the case of horror movies usually comes to life again!

In earlier times the subject exerted a more sinister fascination — so-called 'mummy dust' — the powdered remains of dead Egyptians — was thought to be an essential ingredient in many magical spells and medical remedies — a case of the cure being worse than the disease?

This of course led to a great demand for mummies both inside and outside Egypt, and even to an industry of making 'false mummies' to sell to unsuspecting foreigners. This continued well into the 19th century. Even when, at that time, tighter controls were exerted

by the Egyptian authorities, many mummies were still sold on the Black Market, and even some of the mummies that were acquired for museums for scientific purposes were bought clandestinely.

These days, archaeologists and anthropologists have more moral scruples about the way they treat the dead — even those who have been dead for thousands of years. That's one reason why — even though new techniques of analysis can reveal fascinating information, there is some hesitation about carrying out 'autopsies' on too many mummies in an indiscriminate way. Besides the ethical question, there is the practical one that any analysis must involve at least some degree of destruction.

The studies that have been made in recent years have therefore for the most part been of mummies which were already in a poor state of preservation, and the investigators have tried to do the minimum damage possible — taking only tiny samples of tissue for analysis, or using non-destructive means of study such as X rays.

At the end of each study, it is now customary to restore the mummy to a state of 'decent burial'.

In this way, the scientists involved have tried to satisfy both their curiosity and their consciences.

In a moment, I'm going to ask Dr. Albert Simons, a noted expert on Egyptian archaeology, to give us an overview of some recent studies and what they have revealed . . .

UNIT 13

Scientific studies   (2′12″)

Presenter Well, Dr Simons, tell us something about these detailed studies of Egyptian mummies. What exactly went on?

Dr Simons Well, from the 1970s onwards, there have been several studies, and interestingly, they have involved not only archaeologists and anthropologists, as you might expect, but a wide range of other disciplines — doctors, dentists, radiologists, microbiologists (botanists, even, in some cases) — all working together using their different skills to build up as a complete a picture as possible of what the average Egyptian was like.

Presenter Could you give us an idea of where these studies were made?

Dr Simons Yes, well, the best known were made in Detroit in the early 1970s, Manchester in 1975, and Paris in 1976 — that's the one I'd like to look at in more detail later on . . .

Presenter Fine. What is the particular interest of that investigation?

Dr Simons Well, partly the personage involved — the only actual pharaoh to be studied so far . . .

Presenter Who was he?

Dr Simons His name was Rameses the Second, who is known to have been the third pharaoh of the nineteenth Dynasty — but he's not interesting just because he was a king, some fascinating discoveries were made during the Paris study — some of them rather amusing in a bizarre sort of way — and his body seems to have undergone quite a few adventures since his death. But perhaps first we should get back to the more general discussion of all the studies first.

Presenter Right. So what were the main areas of interest?

Dr Simons Well, there were three main things really. Obviously people wanted to find out as much as possible about the medical condition of the Ancient Egyptians — what diseases they had, the average age of death and that sort of thing. Then, more generally, their physical appearance — height, weight, overall build — even their facial features. And the other thing which has always fascinated people, was the actual process of mummification — what they did, the substances they used, and so on.

Presenter Fine. So perhaps now we could get down to more detail, especially about Rameses and the adventures you said he had undergone.

UNIT 14

Rameses II (6'09")

Dr Simons Well, as I said, there were three areas of interest, so perhaps we should take each in turn.

Presenter Fine. Let's take the medical and physical evidence first.

Dr Simons Mm. Well first of all, life expectancy. Although some very old individuals *were encountered*, and R-Rameses is a case in point — he was probably over 90! (Good Lord!). It seemed the average Egyptian died rather young. From about 30 to 35 years old on the whole, although the nobility, as might be expected, tended to live longer — some of them *have been found to be* 50 or 60 years old.

Well, naturally, the older they got the more medical problems *were encountered*, but some modern disorders *have* so far *not been found*. There is no evidence yet of any malignant tumours, for example, although the fact that most of the people studied were comparatively young could account for this. Another modern problem — dental decay — was also absent, probably due to the plain diet and absence of sugar, though there was another problem with the teeth caused by this same diet. The stones on which their flour *was ground* caused a lot of grit to get into the bread and this eroded the teeth — so much that many older people must have suffered greatly and *could have been confined* to a liquid diet. An abscess on the jaw caused by this kind of erosion may in fact have contributed to the death of Rameses the Second. Analysis of the internal organs of several mummies has revealed that intestinal parasites

were common, even among the upper classes [Really] — evidence of a generally low standard of public hygiene. And another widespread disorder was a form of anaemia. Naturally, the Ancient Egyptians didn't smoke, but er lesions of the lungs were widespread. These, however, are the sort that we associate today with workers in mines and quarries, and must be due in the case of the Egyptians, to living in sandy desert conditions. (Hm) Actually — on the smoking issue — there was a a temporary sensation when traces of what appeared to be tobacco *were found* in Rameses' sarcophagus! But, er botanists later confirmed that it was not in fact tobacco itself, but a related plant which is native to Egypt. In the meantime, the cynics were commenting that it probably had come from the cigarette of some careless Egyptologist or museum attendant of the past!

Presenter Hah, hah and what about their physical appearance?

Dr Simons Well, very much what you would expect from seeing Egyptian art. They were light and slight in build. The average height for both men and women was about 1 metre 60 — and er studies of the skeletons from which the covering of flesh can be extrapolated suggest that they weighed much less in relation to their height than most modern people — from about 10 to 15 kilograms less than someone of a similar height today is the estimate.

Presenter And what about mummification?

Dr Simons Ah well, the first thing to be said is that *it wasn't always done* in the same way and it was by no means infallible, as many people tend to think. Many bodies — including that of the famous king Tutankhamun *were almost entirely destroyed* by overuse of one or other of the substances generally employed. The basic procedure was much the same however — most of the internal organs, including the brain, *were removed* and *preserved* separately in a jar. The brain *was got out* through the nose (uh) using a sort of hook.

Presenter Oh dear!

Dr Simons Yes. It used to be thought that the heart *was always removed* too, but in the case of Rameses *it was found* in place. The body *was then immersed* in a substance called natron — that's a form of sodium carbonate —, which occurs naturally in Egypt — for 40 to 70 days. *It was then washed, made up and wrapped* in linen bandages and *placed* in its coffin or sarcophagus. Then *it was soaked* in oils, resins and perfumes to help preserve it further.

Presenter You said the body *was made up*. Do you mean its face *was painted*?

Dr Simons Yes. Yes Rameses *was not only made up*, they had to restructure his nose, which *was damaged* when they took out his brain (uh). The investigators found that *it had been stuffed* with small animal bones — and er peppercorns of all things! His hair *had been dyed too*.

Presenter You said that Rameses had suffered other adventures after his death?

Dr Simons Ah, well, yes, poor chap. Well, for a start, *he*

was found in a much later tomb than his real date, along with a lot of other Pharoahs and it looks very much as if the priests of later times had moved and reburied him to save him from the tomb robbers. His body *was transported* along with the other pharaohs found in the same tomb, to the Cairo museum — that was in 1871 — and *it was put* on display. Well naturally, removed from the dry desert atmosphere, his body started to deteriorate and by the 1970s was in a very poor state. That was part of the reason why the Egyptian authorities gave their consent for its temporary removal to Paris for the study — yet another upheaval! (Yes). The French experts aimed not only to carry out an investigation, but were also able to apply the latest techniques of restoration and conservation, so that at the end of the study Rameses *was specially treated*, and then *rewrapped* in new bandages — well they weren't exactly new since they were of ancient Egyptian date — *given* a 'new' sarcophagus and carefully *transported* back to Cairo where *he is now kept* in a controlled environment which should slow down the deterioration process.

Presenter So, as I said at the beginning, not only *was* science *served*, but a proper respect *was paid* to the remains in the end.

Dr Simons Exactly.

UNIT 15

The tree climbers of Pompeii (3′39″)

Shelagh um It's another one of my adventures as a tourist um finding out things you really didn't expect to find out when you went to the place! I went to Pompeii and of course what you go to Pompeii for is er the archaeology.

Liz To see the ruins.

Shelagh To see the ruins. And I was actually seeing the ruins but um suddenly my attention was caught by something else. I was just walking round the corner of a ruin, into a group of trees, pine trees, and I was just looking at them, admiring them and suddenly I saw a man halfway up this tree, and I was looking at him so all I could see was his hands and his feet and he was about 20 or 30 feet up. I thought, 'Goodness, what's going on here. Has he got a ladder or hasn't he?' So I walked round to see if he had a ladder. No, he had just gone straight up the tree.

Liz He'd shinned up the tree.

Shelagh He'd shinned up the tree. Like a monkey, more or less, except he was a rather middle-aged monkey . . . He was er he was all of 50 and (Oh God), what's going on here? Anyway, I walked a bit further and saw other people either up trees or preparing to go up trees, and then I noticed a man standing there directing them, a sort of foreman, and began to wonder what on earth was going on, and then on the ground I saw there were all these polythene buckets and they were full of pine cones and of course what they were doing was

collecting pine cones, and I thought, 'Well, how tidy of them to collect pine cones to stop the ruins being um made um made untidy with all these things.' Then I saw there was a lorry . . . full of pine cones . . . This was getting ridiculous . . . They were really collecting them in a big way. So I um asked the er foreman what was going on and he said, 'Well you know um pine nuts are extremely sought after and valuable in the food industry in Italy.'

Liz For food (Yeah). Not fuel! I thought you were going to say they were going to put (burn) them on a fire. Yes.

Shelagh Well, they might burn the er cones when they've finished with them but inside these cones are little white things like nuts and er I realized that they're used in Italian cooking quite a lot in er there's a particular sauce that goes with spaghetti em from Genova, I think, called 'pesto' in which these nuts are ground up and of course they they come in cakes and sweets and things like that.

Liz So it's quite a delicacy.

Shelagh It's quite a delicacy. And of course I'd never thought of how they actually got them 'cos you can't imagine having a pine nut farm. So what he said happens is that private firms like his buy a licence off the Italian State for the right to go round places like Pompeii — archaeological sites and things — and systematically collect all the pine cones that come off the trees and similarly in the in the forests.

Liz And of course they have to go up the tree because by the time it's fallen the the food isn't any good.

Shelagh That's right. They're pulling them down and he said they were very good at um recognizing which ones were ready and which ones were a bit hard and etc. and each of them had a sort of stick with a hook at the end which they were using to pull the pines off, off the trees but clearly it wasn't enough to sit around and wait till they fell down. You, you had to do something about it. There they were. So that was er the end of my looking at the ruins for about half an hour. I was too fascinated by this er strange form of er agriculture.

Liz Well, what you don't intend to see is always the most interesting.

Shelagh Much more interesting.

Worksheet 1   Unit 5 (Home computers)

Use Part 1 and Part 2 (Section 1 of each only)

Divide the class into two groups, A and B. Group A listens to Part 1. Group B listens to Part 2.

Students listen and fill in their worksheets individually.

Students then form pairs or small groups with people who have listened to the same recording as them. They discuss their answers and listen to the recording again to check answers, fill in gaps, etc.

Re-organize the class into 'mixed' groups (students from both group A and B). Students discuss their worksheets again and note any differences between A and B answers.

Finally, the whole class listens to both versions and discusses how they differ in style, in difficulty, etc.

Worksheet 2   Unit 5 (Home computers) and Unit 11 (My computer makes me sick!)

Use Part 1 or Part 2 of Unit 5 and all of Unit 11.

Follow the same procedure as for Worksheet 1.

Worksheet 3   Unit 8 (Bottoms up!) and Unit 15 (The tree climbers of Pompeii)

Use The whole recording for each unit.

Follow the same procedure as for Worksheet 1.

Worksheet 4   Unit 12 (Mummy Dust), Unit 13 (Scientific studies) and Unit 14 (Rameses II)

Use the whole recording for each unit.

Divide the class into two groups. Each group listens to one of the recordings.

Students then form pairs or smaller groups to discuss their answers.

When students are reasonably happy with their answers, they form new groups which should contain at least one person from the original groups. They pool the information they have gathered to produce as much information about the study of Egyptian mummies as possible.

The whole interview (Units 12–14) can then be played through at one sitting to the whole class. (This may take place in a subsequent lesson if time is short.)

WORKSHEETS FOR JIGSAW LISTENING

Worksheet 1   Unit 5 (Home computers)

1   The woman says there are three types of home computer owner. Fill in the chart with the names she gives them and write notes on the way she says they behave.

	Type of owner	Typical behaviour
1		
2		
3		

2   What type of owner does she say she is now?

. . . .

3   She tried to write a program once, and it went very wrong. Take notes on:

a   what she wanted the program to do

b   what went wrong.

4   Write down your own impressions of the situation in which the woman is telling her story, and what you think her mood is at the moment. Here are some ideas to help you, but you can add any of your own. Try to collect evidence for your opinions.

Situation	Evidence	Mood (you can choose more than one)
☐ at a party ☐ sitting at the dinner table ☐ in a radio interview ☐ in quiet conversation with a friend ☐ giving a lecture ☐ your own ideas?		☐ excited ☐ depressed ☐ happy ☐ regretful ☐ resentful ☐ trying to amuse ☐ trying to inform ☐ your own ideas? . . . .

Worksheet 2 Unit 5 (Home computers) and Unit 11 (My computer makes me sick!)

1 The speaker mentions some benefits of using computers and also some of the disadvantages or dangers. Listen to your tape and take notes in the appropriate column.

Benefits	Disadvantages or dangers

2 Is the speaker you heard an expert or an amateur? Write down what you think and add any evidence that justifies your choice.

. . . .

. . . .

3 What is the situation in which the speaker is talking? Choose one alternative and write down any evidence you find to support your choice.

Situation	Evidence
☐ public lecture	
☐ conversation between friends	
☐ radio interview	
☐ radio talk	
☐ seminar for non-experts	

Worksheet 3   Unit 8 (Bottoms up!) and Unit 15 (The tree climbers of Pompeii)

1   Fill in as many of the details as you can about time, place and what the speaker saw.

	Country	*City*	*Specific place*	*Other details*
Where the incident happened				
When the incident happened				
Who the speaker saw				
What they were doing				

2   An item of food is mentioned in the story. What is it, and what is its use in cooking?

. . . .

. . . .

. . . .

Worksheet 4   Unit 12 (Mummy Dust), Unit 13 (Scientific studies) and Unit 14 (Rameses II)

1   Which part of the programme do you think you heard? — the
    first, the middle, or the end part? Write down your choice and add
    any evidence you can to justify it.

                            Evidence

. . . .

                                     . . . .

                                     . . . .

                                     . . . .

2   Take free notes on all the pieces of information that are given
    about Ancient Egypt and the Egyptians themselves.

    . . . .

    . . . .

    . . . .

    . . . .

    . . . .